Ballet Rambert: 50 years and on

Ballet Rambert: 50 years and on

Edited by
Clement Crisp
Anya Sainsbury
Peter Williams

To Dame Marie Rambert and all her artists:

the pioneers of yesterday and today

First printed in Great Britain by the Scolar Press 1976
Revised and enlarged edition 1981

Contents

COVER *Farandole* by Henri Matisse

Acknowledgements

This book would not have been possible without the unfailing help
and encouragement of the following people, all of them associated with
Ballet Rambert during some part of its fifty years:

Sir Frederick Ashton, William Chappell, John Chesworth, Mary Clarke, Agnes de Mille,
Dame Ninette de Valois, Sally Gilmour, Walter Gore, Diana Gould Menuhin,
Nigel Gosling, Maude Lloyd, Dame Alicia Markova, P. W. Manchester,
Norman Morrice, Dame Peggy Van Praagh, Antony Tudor, Sir Sacheverell Sitwell.

To Lord Snowdon go our most grateful thanks for the
portraits of Dame Marie Rambert.

Valerie Bourne, Prudence Skene, John Webley, Susan Robertson
and all at Ballet Rambert were unfailing in their help, and
Philip Dyer was, as always, most helpful with research.
To Leslie Edwards our grateful thanks for loaning his photographs,
and to Madame Georges Duthuit our gratitude for her permission to
reproduce the drawing 'Farandole' by her father, Henri Matisse; and
to Victor Waddington gratitude for his kindness in obtaining the print.
We would like to thank David and Angela Ellis for permission to
reproduce material in their possession, the BBC Hulton Picture Library,
the Theatre Museum Archives, Dame Marie Rambert and the Ballet Rambert Archives
for making available many of the photographs. The David Thomas picture history of
Ballet Rambert in 1951 is reproduced by kind permission of Richard Buckle.

Photographs used in this book include the work of the following photographers

Allegro Studios	Peggy Delius	David Buckland
Gordon Anthony	Malcolm Dunbar	Nobby Clark
John Baker	H. Heidersberger	Boyan Coren
Baron	Angus McBean	Malcolm Hoare
John Blomfield	Duncan Melvin	Eleni Leoussi
Anthony Crickmay	J. D. O'Callaghan	Michael Stannard
Pollard Crowther	Bertram Park	
Alan Cunliffe	Houston Rogers	
Frederika Davis	R. Wilsher	
J. W. Debenham	Paul Wilson	

Reproductions of original costume and set designs from the collections of
Dame Marie Rambert, Maude Lloyd and Ballet Rambert
are by Brook Tellar Limited

The choreographer of the ballet is given in brackets in each caption.

Ballet Rambert is indebted to the generosity and support of the following sponsors:

Commercial Union Assurance Company Limited
Imperial Foods Limited
J. Lyons Group of Companies
R. Alistair McAlpine
Rank Hovis McDougall Limited
Sir Max Rayne
Rowe & Pitman, Hurst-Brown
J. Sainsbury Limited
Sotheby Parke Bernet & Company
United Biscuits
S. G. Warburg & Company

all of whom contributed to the first edition of this
publication, and to Lady Charlotte Bonham-Carter and
the Linbury Trust who made this second edition possible.

Proceeds from the sale of this book will be given to Ballet Rambert.

In the 50th and Golden Year

Sacheverell Sitwell

Ballet Rambert now in its incredible fiftieth year amounts to an astonishing personal achievement. Many talents have been variously engaged in it, but throughout there has been the indomitable, unconquerable Marie Rambert, herself, in person. Now become in truth one of the legendary figures of our day. For all the years she has been inspirer and commander, never flinching in upholding her standards of taste and supporting her beloved enterprise in times alike of storm and doldrum. Her dedication, bravery and devotion to duty have been beyond all commendation. Fearless, and ever 'steady in the line', to apply a military term of praise and encomium to her. Not that someone of her fine temperament and sensibility must not have had her moods of exaltation and despair, but her fiery energy, her persistence, her personal charm and humour time and again have produced success when all the odds seemed set against her. Thinking back over the years her achievement appears almost inconceivable. For there have been times when it seemed quite out of the question that it could continue. In those early days there was no Arts Council to lend out a helping hand. But here it is still, young in repertoire and if anything more controversial than ever.

Ballet Rambert has always been the nursery of young and budding talents. Frederick Ashton, greatest of living choreographers, had his beginnings in the now historic little theatre in Notting Hill. Ninette de Valois produced here her *Bar aux Folies Bergère*, and Andrée Howard was another of the young talents at work there. The rest of this little piece I am trying to write in homage to 'Mim' as she is known to those who love her, could consist of nothing other than a list of names of those who had their first applause in her aegis, under her wing. How much, too, as a person she loves poetry! And there were certainly moments of that in her little theatre. Pearl Argyle, who died tragically so young ,was the muse of poetry in person. How I would love Herrick, or Antoine Watteau to have seen her on that little stage in *Mermaid*! She used to read my poems in the tube. And now all these years later this memory is an inspiration to me to continue. I am sure I am not the only person to whom that theatre precinct is not a little haunted.

There can be but few of the huge public of today who realize the apparent collapse of the ballet tradition after Diaghilev died in 1929. Marie Rambert, it is true, was by then already out at sea in her lifeboat looking for survivors. And it is probably due to her in the first place that the slow revival came, grown by now into a vast and increasing public. Lovers of ballet will always remember her for this. What a spate of energy spread over such a stretch of years and the emanation of so diminutive a figure! With such a character, all her own: generous, loyal, impulsive, cajoling, wheedling, and sure almost always to get her own way in the end! And it comes to this, that we have still with us the friend of the immortal Vaslav Nijinsky–in all likelihood the only true woman friend who understood him and had sympathy with him in his difficulties–in the fiftieth and golden year, for her jubilee has more than a little of a golden wedding in it, of the ballet company she has kept going through thick and thin for most of the years of a long lifetime. All honour to her for this! And the grateful affection, I know I can say, of her dancers and her public.

Movement is my element

MARIE RAMBERT
talks to Peter Williams

Photographs Snowdon

Fifty years ago, at the time when you were all involved in
A Tragedy of Fashion *at the Lyric, Hammersmith,*
did you have any idea at all that one day you might become
something like a national monument?

I hadn't the remotest idea and I have never thought
of the future. That's why the present always
escapes me and only the past remains. Somehow
when it's all past, it seems something has been done.
But neither at the moment when it was being done
did I realise what I did, nor can I think of the
future, it's absolutely beyond me.

Didn't your time with Diaghilev ever give you an idea
of what you might want to do?

I'm afraid, no! It is an awful shortcoming in my
nature that I cannot look into the future, maybe
because I am frightened; I am a dreadful coward.
When I left Diaghilev I had some vague ideas that I
would do dance evenings and so on, but it may have
been something Nijinsky said to me that possibly
planted the seed. I had more than one serious talk
with him, during those three weeks we were alone
without Diaghilev in Monte Carlo, it may have been
from these conversations that he said 'This is not a
company for you, it is all too big, you need something different'. As you know Nijinsky was not very
articulate and he couldn't find the words but
possibly what he said was a sort of grain that eventually grew.

I wouldn't have thought it was so much a question
of your being afraid of the future as of your being inspired
by the present.

I would love to use the word 'inspired' but I think
that I work instinctively; the fact that I never
became a dancer was predestined. I was longing to
be a dancer but I didn't have the physical attributes,

specially for a classical dancer. But I always had the enormous desire to express myself through movement and not being able to do it well enough through my own movement maybe led me gradually to form a company. But when I say form a company, it started in such an indefinite way. For instance when I started my school, in about 1920, as soon as I saw the pupils I felt they were material in my hands when I had a class; I wanted to make them dance in addition to exercises. So I taught them what I remembered from Diaghilev's time; I remembered, for instance, all the variations from *The Sleeping Princess* which I taught to the girls; I was very anxious to get it better and better and I knew quite instinctively how it should be done. Although I myself had never danced these variations on the stage I felt absolutely the way they should be done. Even when my two daughters, Angela and Lulu, were very small and they had a party I would make my best pupils dance – Pearl Argyle or Andrée Howard, for instance, would dance one of the variations. We did things like that and it would probably have continued in that way because unless I get a push I don't move. I don't move, that is, towards the future but I move non-stop in other directions. Movement is my element, of that I'm absolutely sure.

What then was it that really did make you move towards the future?

Well, in '25, my husband Ashley Dukes, had a tremendous success with his play, *The Man with a Load of Mischief* and began to think about building a theatre. He became very fashionable having had this success at the Haymarket, so it wasn't I who was the cause of Nigel Playfair inviting me to make a ballet; he happened to ask me one evening in the theatre 'And what are you doing in your studio?', I replied 'We are working now on a little ballet for which Ashley gave us an idea'. It was because of Ashley that Playfair came to the studio.

What was the idea that Ashley gave you?

We were having a holiday in Normandy and Ashley, as always, was reading a lot of French books and he

read in Madame de Sévigné the story of the cook of
some Duke who was expecting the King, Louis XIV,
to dinner. He had a wonderful cook, Vatel, and the
fish didn't arrive from Dieppe in time to make a
dish fit for a king. When the fish finally arrived they
went to look for Vatel and found him hanging in his
garret; he couldn't bear the shame of having failed
the King. Ashley thought it a good idea for ballet
and I thought so too, but Massine had done a ballet
with knives, forks and food in *The Good-Humoured
Ladies* so perhaps we could do the same thing with
dress-making. Now at that time I had a friend,
Sophie Fedorovitch, whom I had met four years
before during the rehearsals of Diaghilev's *Sleeping
Princess*, so I thought if Sophie could do the décor
then another pupil of mine, Frances James, who
had done some small works at that time, could do
the choreography for this ballet. I also had at this
time one male pupil who had been sent to me by
Massine, Frederick Ashton; he seemed inattentive in
that he couldn't pick up a combination of steps but I
think he was feeling something different in his body
which was in the way of picking up these steps.
Anyway he was the only male pupil I had so he was
the only person to dance the male part in this ballet,
but he didn't even want to dance it since he felt he
wasn't ready. However, after I persuaded him he
came to me and said that he had been thinking about
the part, Monsieur Duchic, and how he tortures his
brains to think of how he can create these dresses,
and then he began to do movements which were so
beautiful and so chic and so absolutely right in the
way that his head and shoulders were properly
turned. Everything looked right so I said to him
'You will have to do this ballet' but he refused
because he said he had never done anything like
that and that he was only a beginner. So I said that
I was sure that he could do it and that I would be
able to help him. At last I persuaded him; then I said,
'What music do you want?' and he said that we
must ask Poulenc or Auric but I said that we couldn't
afford them; also because he didn't yet know the
shape, and the music must give him the shape, we
must have music that already existed. Then he said
that for costumes and set we must have Chanel;

again I refused because I said we couldn't afford her and also the only mistake that Diaghilev ever made was to have a chic dressmaker who made dresses for elegant women when he did *Le Train Bleu*; it had nothing to do with the stage. So for music, after looking everywhere I found a suite by Eugene Goossens, then Diaghilev's conductor; for the designer I told him about my friend Sophie Fedorovitch and when they met it was love at first sight for all her life.

So when I found this Goossens music I began to arrange a dance myself and immediately Fred jumped up and said 'Not like that', then he showed me something entirely different. I immediately saw that he could arrange dances; then once he really started, his imagination was fantastic, every day he came with new ideas. Such splendid ideas and, for one thing, as soon as he saw the design for Frances James, a beautiful pink satin dress with an enormous bow hanging down to the ground, he said she must come in with her back to the audience and bourrée along the backcloth. Another thing, I said presumably Vatel would have killed himself with his kitchen knife, so Fred said 'I will kill myself with my scissors'. I rejoiced all the time as he had such wonderful ideas. Then I said to him that I felt the finish was so sad, with a suicide, so he said 'well, we will bring on the mannequins' and he did an ensemble for them to the dirge music. It was

extraordinary, in this his second year, he was so
predestined to be a choreographer; at that time all
he wanted was to become the premier danseur of
the great world, a sort of male Pavlova who was
the first person to inspire him. His real vocation was
to be a great choreographer while mine was teaching.

So after the success of A Tragedy of Fashion
in the revue, Riverside Nights, *this then led naturally
to the Ballet Club?*

Actually, after some performances of my Rambert
Dancers, also at the Lyric Hammersmith, Ashley
felt we should do something permanent since we
already had a theatre which at that time was just
being finished in Ladbroke Road, Notting Hill. So
we formed the Ballet Club in 1930, at the time that
we were still dancing with Karsavina. In the meantime the Camargo Society was formed in London
and their first performances were before the first
performances at the Ballet Club.

*So you totally formed the first generation of
British choreographers?*

Yes. Fred went on working with me until '34; by
that time he had been nearly nine years with me,

not non-stop because he did other things also, but he did ballets for us over this period. Then one day Andrée Howard came to me; she was a very lyrical choreographer, had a sense of comedy and was very musical. She had a remarkable talent; if we had her with us today it would do us all a lot of good. Even before her, in '31, Antony Tudor came to me and said he wanted to do a ballet; he was at that time teaching the children's class and before that he had been working as an accountant in his uncle's business in Smithfield. He couldn't come to class until four in the afternoon and I thought that somebody who has to start at six in the morning and is ready to have a dance class at four is a person of my choice. So he came to me with the idea of the garden scene from *Twelfth Night* which he felt lent itself to ballet; he showed me some movements: there was great logic in his composition and he found music of Frescobaldi, a contemporary of Shakespeare, and the result was his *Cross-Garter'd*. After that he went on and did many ballets for me including his two great masterpieces, *Lilac Garden* and *Dark Elegies*. So we had Andrée and Antony; then there was a day that Walter Gore came to me and said 'Now that you have launched all your infants, may I do a ballet and it won't cost anything at all?' As you know, we were always in a state of penury and it is my pride that Fred's *Capriol Suite* with costumes by Billy Chappell was done for £5 and even our most expensive ballet, *Les Masques* with wonderful designs by Sophie, only cost £60. Anyway I asked Walter what he wanted to do and he wanted to use up Sophie's set for *Valentine's Eve*, which we couldn't do on our small stage since it had been created for the Duke of York's Theatre, and so he used the screens for *Valse Finale*, not very good but I could see that he was a choreographer, and he went on to do some splendid things. Perhaps more than any of the others Walter was a poet of love. Then one day we were trying to remember Susan Salaman's *Le Cricket*, from her *Sporting Sketches* which she did in 1930, and I said to Frank Staff surely he could remember it since he knew how to play cricket; immediately he began to do movements that were much better than real cricket and behold there was somebody with a real talent. So I pushed him and talked to him and he became a choreographer; his *Czernyana* was wit personified but it also had a wonderful lyrical quality.

How did you manage to cajole all these people into doing choreography, presumably you treated them very badly?

I don't think I treated them badly but I must say that I wasn't so much a mother as a midwife. I felt something that can be born is going to be born, and that I helped them to bring it into the world. I knew them very well, I knew their characters and I think that I gave different corrections to every pupil and I feel in that way I was very sensitive. When I felt that they had something creative in them, I think that I then launched them.

After the Ballet Club had been going for some years, it then became Ballet Rambert?

It wasn't my fault. I had a programme, when we did a television, and I called it the Mercury Ballet, but we had an agent and we were going to give a season in the West End and he didn't think the name Mercury Ballet would do at all since it didn't mean anything; he said we must call it Ballet Rambert.

In fact the history of the company falls into separate phases. There was, for instance, the first great creative phase during the Ballet Club days, then there was the less creative phase when the company enlarged and you were doing more full-length classics.

I had to do that because as soon as my choreo-graphers did well for me they got work outside the Ballet Club which was much more lucrative. It broke my heart to part from them but I understood and had to accept it. So I did *Giselle* since I wasn't satisfied with the productions of *Giselle* that I saw in those days and I was longing to do it. It had only two or three main parts, the rest was for corps-de-ballet which we could manage. It had very good notices and I think was generally acclaimed. I longed do more classical ballets, later we did *Don Quixote*, with the Don of all time in John Chesworth, and at that time we had Lucette Aldous who was an adorable Kitri; she was also so very touching in our production of *La Sylphide*. We had a production of *Coppélia*, which brought us great box office success. I am very happy when I think of those classical ballets. I loved to do them and I would have loved to have a big corps-de-ballet, but I think the minimum I had was well produced and was convincing. I am not ashamed of those productions.

It was presumably for economic reasons that the company changed its direction in 1966?

That was not my idea. It came from a pupil of mine who came to me twenty-four years ago and Norman Morrice went on to become one of my splendid choreographers. Well, in the mid-'sixties it was becoming terribly difficult because we never had a proper orchestra and the provinces only wanted to see the classics. I suffered terribly from penury although it taught me to exploit every penny that was given, which in a way was splendid because it meant less material and more feeling and brain. So I must thank God for having been poor. Norman came to me one day and suggested that this way of dragging around a corps-de-ballet and trying to do classics in an impoverished way was not working since we were always being compared with all these big companies who seemed to abound at that time. So he suggested that we should keep a company only of soloists – no stars, no corps, just soloists. He found that, after he had done his third ballet for the company, the corps was an unnecessary thing and only a drag on the company. It was entirely Norman's idea to alter the shape of the company and from that moment I became a looker-on.

You will never, never be only a looker-on.

I was still a director and this comes from Norman's kindness and respect for me and he consulted me about everything at the beginning. I soon felt that his way of saying things, his gestures and his completely modern outlook was not the way that my own imagination worked. I couldn't really direct that, though after I had seen a ballet a few times I understood why it was done, so I felt that he really should direct the company. But with his courtesy, sensitiveness and also the trust he had in my judgement, he always talked to me about everything that I could express an opinion about. I was very happy but unfortunately it meant that he overworked for eight years. In this time he succeeded in re-forming the company.

Well now you know everything that happens today and we are so lucky to have other pupils of the Rambert school, John Chesworth, who is now Director, with Christopher Bruce as Associate Director. The awful thing is that for a moment I couldn't remember their names, but I have an awful memory for names even forgetting, the other day, what my daughter was called; in other respects my memory is pretty good and I can, as you know, remember perfectly the forty sonnets of Shakespeare, and that is not to be snuffed at – I mean sneezed at. But all this helps me in my sleepless nights and I think I can remember details of all the ballets I have seen.

Looking back on that fifty years, what is the thing you are most proud of?

My choreographers. They trusted me; we fought but they trusted me and I like to think that they have greatly enriched the English repertory and they were, and are, very important people. I am deeply grateful to them, wherever they are now and for whom ever they work.

'... from this theatre of
150 yellow velvet seats
came all that was best in ballet'
Walter Gore.

'It was in this shoe-box ...
that the renaissance of
English dance occurred'
Agnes de Mille.

The first forty years

Mary Clarke

I was not yet three years old when '*A Tragedy of Fashion*' was first produced and a date could be established for the beginning of Ballet Rambert. My credentials for writing this article were given to me by Dame Marie Rambert when she invited me to write a book about her company and promised all the help she could give. I had to do the research and I consulted very many people who had seen all or nearly all of the work of the company in its early days. But it was the sessions with Rambert herself which brought most vividly to life the tiny beginnings, the struggles and the achievements of the company. Working with her–she had an extraordinary gift for talking in 'chapters', each time she said 'Let us stop, I am tired' we had come to a natural break–I felt that I too had studied under Madame Mercury. I had experienced for myself the incredible enthusiasm and the deep culture that goaded and nurtured her first dancers and choreographers. Above all, I learned her gift for encouragement, her spontaneous expression of approval, not necessarily for any work I had done but her reactions to new ballets, new dancers, plays in the World Theatre series, new discoveries she made in reading. She must have fed these enthusiasms and this enormous range of interests back to her company. I think the only difference between our sessions and the work done at the Mercury Theatre in the 1930s was that there were never any rows. Madame Mercury obviously felt less passionately about my prose than she did about the perfection of the classic dance. Never did she have to scream 'But you have ruined, absolutely *ruined* the choreography of Fokine'.

Before describing the work of Ballet Rambert it is important to sketch the background. Dame Marie Rambert was born Cyvia Rambam in Warsaw in

1888 of mixed Polish and Russian blood. Her parents were booksellers and wide reading was something taken absolutely for granted in the household. Rambert (as she eventually called herself) learned a kind of mixture of ballet and social dancing at her High School and was deeply moved by seeing a performance by Isadora Duncan in Warsaw but had no thought then of becoming a dancer. In 1905, alarmed by her involvement in revolutionary activities, her parents suggested she go to Paris to study medicine and it was in Paris that she discovered a natural talent to improvise and compose dances which were well received at fashionable houses. Isadora's brother Raymond praised her work. In 1910, at the suggestion of a friend, she went to study at the Summer School of Emile Jaques-Dalcroze in Switzerland and enjoyed his teaching so much that she stayed three years. She left in 1913 when, on the recommendation of 'Monsieur Jaques', she was engaged by Serge Diaghilev to help Vaslav Nijinsky count the difficult rhythms of Stravinsky's *Le Sacre du Printemps* for which he was preparing the choreography. She was used in various ballets in the repertory, usually in the back row as she then had little technique and little interest in classical ballet. She was absorbed in the new style of dance being invented by Nijinsky for *Sacre*. She went with the company on the South American tour of 1913 (during which Nijinsky got married) and on board ship suddenly understood the beauty of the classic style as she watched the great ballerina Tamara Karsavina at practice. She used to toil away in the heat, learning all she could from Karsavina's example. Karsavina called her 'my little black shadow' and they formed a friendship which has lasted until today and which was greatly to help Ballet Rambert in the years ahead.

After the South American tour, Rambert was not re-engaged by Diaghilev. She gave more recitals in Paris and on the outbreak of war in 1914 made her escape to England, travelling on the same steamer as Chaliapin. She had no private means and supported herself to begin with by teaching eurhythmics (which she had learned with Dalcroze). She also gave dancing lessons in private houses and

. to find me on stage
had to look for
large insteps and a nose'.
derick Ashton.

nt Row, from left to
t: Robert Stuart,
iam Chappell, Pearl
yle, Frederick Ashton,
rée Howard, Diana
uld. Back Row: Marie
bert, Prudence
nan, Arnold Haskell

This (Saturday) Evening, December 20th, at 8.15
Subsequent Evenings at 8.45
(For Three Weeks only)

NIGEL PLAYFAIR presents
(By arrangement with MARIE RAMBERT)

A Christmas Season of Ballet

I.
CARNAVAL

Ballet by FOKINE.   Music by SCHUMANN.   Costumes by BAKST.

Columbine .... THAMAR KARSAVINA
Harlequin .... LEON WOIZIKOWSKY
Estrella (in Pink) .... MARIE RAMBERT
Florestan .... HAROLD TURNER
Chiarina } (in Blue) .... DIANA GOULD
Eusebius .... FREDERICK ASHTON
Papillon .... ANDRÉE HOWARD
Pierrot .... ROBERT STUART
Pantalon .... WALTER GORE
First Lady in White .... PEARL ARGYLE
Second Lady in White .... PRUDENCE HYMAN
First Guest .... WILLIAM CHAPPELL
Second Guest .... ANTHONY TUDOR

Produced by LEON WOILIKOWSKY.

II.
SPORTING SKETCHES

By SUSAN SALAMAN

A.—CRICKET.

Fielders.. DIANA GOULD, ELIZABETH SCHOOLING and MAUD LLOYD
The Batsman .... WILLIAM CHAPPELL
The Bowler .... ANTHONY TUDOR
The Umpire .... ROBERT STUART

B.—RUGBY.

The Rugby Player .... HAROLD TURNER
His "Fans" .... PEARL ARGYLE, ANDRÉE HOWARD and
PRUDENCE HYMAN

INTERVAL 8 MINUTES.

III.
A FLORENTINE PICTURE

Groupings by FREDERICK ASHTON.   Music by CORELLI.

The Madonna .... MARIE RAMBERT
Angels ...... DIANA GOULD, PEARL ARGYLE, ANDRÉE HOWARD,
PRUDENCE HYMAN, ELIZABETH SCHOOLING
and MAUD LLOYD

IV.
LE SPECTRE DE LA ROSE

Ballet by FOKINE.   Music by WEBER.   Costumes by BAKST.

The Young Girl .... THAMAR KARSAVINA
Spirit of the Rose .... HAROLD TURNER

INTERVAL 10 MINUTES.

V.
LES SYLPHIDES

Ballet by FOKINE.   Music by CHOPIN.

(1) Nocturne....THAMAR KARSAVINA, DIANA GOULD, FREDERICK
ASHTON and Misses ARGYLE, HYMAN, SCHOOLING,
LLOYD, CUFF, MORFIELD and FLECK
(2) Mazurka .... PRUDENCE HYMAN
(3) Valse .... THAMAR KARSAVINA
(4) Mazurka .... FREDERICK ASHTON
(5) Prelude .... PEARL ARGYLE
(6) Valse....THAMAR KARSAVINA and FREDERICK ASHTON
(7) Grande Valse .... ENSEMBLE

VI.
CAPRIOL SUITE

Ballet by FREDERICK ASHTON.   Music by PETER WARLOCK.
Costumes by WILLIAM CHAPPELL.

(1) Basse Dance.....PEARL ARGYLE, PRUDENCE HYMAN, WILLIAM
CHAPPELL, ROBERT STUART
(2) Pavane......DIANA GOULD, FREDERICK ASHTON and HAROLD
TURNER
(3) Sordion........ANDRÉE HOWARD and HAROLD TURNER
(4) Mattachins...FREDERICK ASHTON, HAROLD TURNER, WILLIAM
CHAPPELL, ROBERT STUART
(5) Pieds-en-L'air.....DIANA GOULD, PEARL ARGYLE, FREDERICK
ASHTON, WILLIAM CHAPPELL
(6) Branles .... ENSEMBLE

VII.
DIVERTISSEMENT

(1) Shepherd's Hornpipe (arranged by Balanchin)........Handel
LEON WOIZIKOWSKY
(2) Fairy Tales from "The Sleeping Beauty"........Tchaikowsky
(a) Porcelain Princesses
S. MORFIELD   B. CUFF   C. FLECK
(b) Blue Bird and Prince
PRUDENCE HYMAN   HAROLD TURNER
(c) Sugar Plum Fairy (arranged by Petipas)
PEARL ARGYLE
(d) Red Riding Hood (arranged by Petipas)
The Wolf....................ROBERT STUART
Red Riding Hood....SUZETTE MORFIELD
(3) Mannequin (arranged by F. Ashton)................Goossens
DIANA GOULD
(4) Farrucca (arranged by Massine)................... de Falla
LEON WOIZIKOWSKY
(5) Final Galop .... Strauss
THE WHOLE COMPANY

Programme of the 1930 Christmas Season given by
The Ballet Club at the Lyric Theatre, Hammersmith.

The Lady of Shalott
with Pearl Argyle
and Maude Lloyd as
the Lady and her Reflection,
Susette Morfield, on stairs,
Tamara Svetlova, Leslie
Edwards, Elizabeth Schooling,
Frank Staff and Anne Gee.
[ASHTON]

June Brae and Harold Turner in *Lysistrata*.
[TUDOR]

Tamara Karsavina and Harold Turner in *Les Sylphides*
with the Rambert Dancers.   [FOKINE]

taught one group of politicians' children in White-
hall. But she was restless. The Diaghilev Ballet was
stranded in Spain. The London theatre offered
mostly 'light entertainment' for troops on leave.
Then through a friend of her Paris days, Vera
Donnet (later Vera Bowen), she was asked in 1917
to create a ballet, *La Pomme d'Or*, for a Sunday night
performance put on by the Stage Society. Stage
Society audiences then were rather like Royal Court
ones today and to have a success was to make your
name. Rambert did and C. B. Cochran gave the
ballet another showing.

By this time Rambert was the subject of press in-
terviews and much in demand at dinner parties
where her quick wit, erudition and sense of humour
enlivened any gathering. At one such, later in 1917
she met the playwright Ashley Dukes and they were
married on 3 March 1918. Dukes was not only an
important and very successful man in the British
theatre but also an authority on European drama.
Rambert's marriage contributed much to her work;
because of Ashley, her intellectual and artistic hori-
zon was kept wide and she never became suffocated
in the rarefied world of ballet.

She started teaching ballet in 1920 in her own
studio but continued to study herself with such
pedagogues as Astafieva and Cecchetti, delighting
especially in those months when the Diaghilev
Ballet was in London and his dancers would all be
in Cecchetti's class. Among her pupils were Diana
and Griselda Gould and in 1924 Frederick Ashton
arrived, sent by Massine. Rambert was not then
staging any ballets or dance entertainments of her
own as teaching (and the birth of two daughters)
occupied her time. She was interested in the ideas of
her pupils and in a little ballet arranged by Frances
James for a charity performance which had costumes designed by Sophie Fedorovitch.

On holiday in France in 1925, Ashley and Rambert toyed with the idea of turning the story of the
chef, Vatel, into a ballet. 'Food' as a subject had
been too recently used by Massine in *Les Femmes
de Bonne Humeur* so they decided to turn the per-
fectionist into a couturier who would kill himself
after the failure of a 'creation'. Back in the studio,

the idea was mooted and discussed and the couturier was give a name. One day Ashton walked in and said 'You know, I think Monsieur Duchic would behave rather like this' and demonstrated an affected walk and nervous gestures. Rambert pounced: '*You must do this ballet*'. 'No, no' said Ashton, but he was persuaded and also persuaded that they could not afford to commission a score from Poulenc or costumes from Chanel. The 'blessed poverty' which, Karsavina once said, forced all the young Rambert artists to use imagination, led in this case to Ashton's introduction to Sophie Fedorovitch as the right designer for him. She was the right designer, and his closest friend until the end of her life; his latest ballet *A Month in the Country* has her name in its dedication.

Having started work, Ashton revealed a true choreographer's approach, thinking always in terms of movement and danced gesture. It was a trifle, but a *chic* and entertaining one and when it was taken into the Nigel Playfair-A.P. Herbert revue *Riverside Nights* at the old Lyric Theatre, Hammersmith on 15 June 1926 it had a distinct success. The name of Ashton was unknown and Rambert was famous as Mrs. Ashley Dukes, wife of the author of the enormously successful play *The Man With a Load of Mischief*. But the quality of the ballet was such that Ninette de Valois went backstage on opening night to congratulate Ashton and to tell Rambert she had found a choreographer. Diaghilev went to see it more than once and it was doubtless because of *A Tragedy of Fashion* that Diaghilev later visited the Rambert studio where he so greatly admired Diana Gould and wanted her for his company when she grew older. (Alas, he died when she was still only sixteen.)

A Tragedy of Fashion did not live in any repertory but its success gave new heart to the Rambert students. The possibility of a native English ballet was still more a dream than a reality but something had been accomplished. All of these young dancers had to earn their living as best they could (mostly in revue or cabaret) and work in the studio for love. In 1927 Ashley Dukes bought the former Horbury Hall at Notting Hill Gate, near his home, and turned

Margot Fonteyn and Frederick Ashton in *Les Sylphides* with the Rambert Dancers.   [FOKINE]

William Chappell, Maude Lloyd (centre) and Pearl Argyle in *The Planets*.   [TUDOR]

(below) A group from *Czernyana* with Celia·Franca, Frank Staff and Walter Gore. [STAFF]

La Fête Etrange with Maude Lloyd as the bride and Frank Staff as the country boy, and David Paltenghi, on the stairs, as the bridegroom.   [HOWARD]

Death and the Maiden: Andrée Howard and John Byron. [HOWARD]

Paris-Soir Celia Franca, Susette Morfield and Maude Lloyd. [GORE]

it in to the Mercury Theatre. In the late 1920s and early 1930s Rambert had among her pupils Andrée Howard, a choreographer and designer of exquisite taste; Maude Lloyd, the lovely South African ballerina; Pearl Argyle, most beautiful of all English dancers; the strong technician and indefatigable worker, Harold Turner; William Chappell, gifted as a designer as well as a dancer; handsome Hugh Laing; and Prudence Hyman of the pure classical line. Walter Gore was soon to join them and become a choreographer of note.

Studio performances were given by these 'Marie Rambert Dancers' but by 1930 Ashton, already the choreographer of many beautiful short works (*Leda and the Swan, Mars and Venus, Les Petits Riens*) thought they were ready for a public matinée. This duly took place at the Lyric Hammersmith on 25 February 1930 and Ashton choreographed his *Capriol Suite*, to music of Peter Warlock, which survived until well into the 1960s.

Ashton had made his point. They were ready for the professional theatre as a company of English dancers, with English choreography to offer.

The success of the matinée was sealed with a two week season at the Lyric in June-July and a three week season at Christmas. Both seasons were 'sell outs' and both were graced by the presence of Karsavina as guest artist. Karsavina had 'borrowed' Harold Turner from Rambert to partner her at some recitals and Nigel Playfair suggested that she might be willing to dance with the company. She accepted Rambert's nervous invitation with pleasure and her presence among the young dancers was an inspiration they none of them ever forgot. 'She blessed us and we flourished', wrote Ashton, 'and we must be for ever grateful for the privilege of touching the fringe of her glory.'

The year 1930 was a watershed in the history of British ballet. Diaghilev had died in the August of 1929 and Pavlova would die in January 1931. The Ballet Russe de Monte Carlo would not get to London until the summer of 1933. In those years British ballet had established itself and could hold its own against the glamorous Russian seasons.

Several of the Diaghilev dancers settled in

London to appear in Massine ballets in Cochran revues. One was Leon Woizikovski who had learned *L'après-midi d'un Faune* from Nijinsky and taught it to the Rambert company. Karsavina taught them *Les Sylphides* and danced *Le Spectre de la Rose* with Harold Turner. Woizikovski also staged *Le Carnaval*. Parallel with these revivals were creations of new ballets from within the company.

An audience had been won and must be kept. Ashley Dukes decided to form the Ballet Club and give Sunday night performances at the Mercury Theatre. The Ballet Club was something special to that era. Its membership list was studded with famous names from society and the arts. Ashley's wine cellar was appreciated in intermissions in what was then the Print Room (housing a remarkable collection of prints of the Romantic Ballet, now in the V & A Museum). In this cultivated but tiny home the Rambert dancers worked all day; there was a remarkable outpouring of creativity.

Andrée Howard made her exquisite *Mermaid* ballet, Ashton was creating for Alicia Markova works like *La Péri, Mephisto Waltz, Les Masques*. Susan Salaman had a success with her *Sporting Sketches*, and by 1931 Antony Tudor was trying his hand at choreography. Ninette de Valois animated Manet's painting *Bar aux Folies Bergère*. Tudor made *Jardin aux Lilas* in 1936 and *Dark Elegies* the following year.

In 1935 Ashton joined the Vic-Wells Ballet as principal choreographer and did very little more work for Rambert. But Tudor's reputation was already made, Andrée Howard's output was considerable and by the late 1930s Walter Gore and Frank Staff were at work. An Andrée Howard ballet of 1939, *Lady into Fox*, a balletic version of David Garnett's novel, made the name of Sally Gilmour, a dancer-actress of great sensitivity who inspired many early ballets by Walter Gore and became a fragile and beautiful Giselle.

The war years were hard for the company but they danced gallantly in factories and canteens and at the Arts Theatre in London where (at the suggestion of Peggy van Praagh) they gave short programmes of '*Lunch Ballet*', '*Tea Ballet*' even '*Sherry*.

Gala Performance with Anna Truscott, Elsa Recagno, and Lucette Aldous. Their cavaliers are Peter Curtis, John Chesworth, and John O'Brien.
[TUDOR]

Ballet' at appropriate hours. After the war, the staging of *Giselle* (designed by Hugh Stevenson) with a perfect understanding of the Romantic style revolutionized the British way of producing old ballets. In 1947 Andrée Howard produced a full length ballet, *The Sailor's Return*, for Gilmour and Gore; John Gilpin had a small part as the Rabbit Catcher.

Then came a tour of Australia, fantastically successful and several times extended in length. It converted many Australians to ballet but it dealt an almost mortal blow to the company. Several dancers (among them Sally Gilmour) settled in Australia; the sets and costumes were lost on the voyage home and the company returned to London nearly bankrupt.

Lucette Aldous in *La Sylphide*.
[BOURNONVILLE]

The Fugitive, a photograph taken on the German tour with David Paltenghi, Mary Munro and Margaret Hill. [HOWARD]

The Descent of Hebe with John Gilpin and Sally Gilmour in a performance just after the war. [TUDOR]

Joyce Graeme as Myrtha in *Giselle* Act II, 1945.
[CORALLI/PERROT]

Phoenix-like, as always, it recovered. Paula Hinton succeeded Gilmour as a powerful theatrical talent and was in turn succeeded by the dazzling Lucette Aldous who danced *Coppélia* and the title role in a lovely staging (by Elsa Marianne von Rosen) of *La Sylphide* in 1960. The 1950s had not been vintage years for new choreography but the production in 1958 of *Two Brothers* introduced an interesting young talent in Norman Morrice. He was to be the mainstay of the company over the next decade and more.

Notable in the fifties was the work of David Ellis who became Associate Director at a time when crisis loomed up in the existence of Ballet Rambert. His decision to devote all his time to working for the company resulted in the suspension of Ballet Workshop, a highly successful venture which he had directed with his wife Angela, Marie Rambert's daughter, for four years at the Mercury Theatre.

New choreography, alas, is not very acceptable to audiences outside London–or, at least, not in those days when the company was trying to pull in a 'general' audience with their full length classics which by 1962 included a staging of *Don Quixote*. The demands of audiences for 'classics', and the crippling cost of mounting them, was putting a strain on Arts Council funding which was becoming unendurable. A change had to be made and the ideas for such change came, typically, from choreographers within the company. No one welcomed the change more open-mindedly or enthusiastically than Dame Marie Rambert, then a mere seventy-eight years young.

In 1966, when it seemed that Ballet Rambert's image as a creative company was fading, the decision was made to return once again to the forefront of creative dance in Britain. Inspired in part by the achievements of Nederlands Dans Theater, Norman Morrice and Marie Rambert re-shaped the company as a group of soloists ready to work in both classic and modern style–a truly creative company as it had originally been.

La Muse s' Amuse: Frank Staff and Andrée Howard.   [HOWARD]

Dark Elegies Sally Gilmour in the 1944 production.   [TUDOR]

Peter and the Wolf cast includes Selma Siegertz, Audrey Nicholls and Terry Gilbert.
[STAFF]

Paula Hinton and John Chesworth in *Sweet Dancer*.
[GORE]

Beryl Goldwyn and Kenneth Bannerman in *Giselle*.   **33**
[CORALLI/PERROT]

A Tragedy of Fashion 1926 Marie Rambert and
Frederick Ashton.   [ASHTON]

From Sir Frederick Ashton

On this great occasion, I would like to shower
Rambert with scented roses (her path is already
strewn with stars of her own making) as a token
for all that she has done for British ballet in the past
fifty years.

For many of those years I must have been a thorn
under her feet and it certainly was quite an under-
taking for her to work up my enthusiasm. I was sent
to her by Leonid Massine, with whom I was then
taking my first classes. I came to her an unpromis-
ing, pimply youth of eighteen, a painfully thin and
self-conscious public-school boy, two profiles stuck
together and a gaping mouth. As my mother said at
the time, to find me on stage one had to look for two
large insteps and a nose. So I became Rambert's
pupil and how she saw any potential in me is hard to
imagine, except that male dancers were a rarity in
those days. However, she managed somehow to
instil some kind of confidence in me and launched
me on my career.

Her tremendous energy was both inspiring and

Frederick Ashton in his *La Péri*, 1931.

an irritant; together we managed to produce many
works. Her great sense of humour (always a delight)
and her wide culture, past associations, and her
incredible memory (which made it possible for her
to quote faultlessly from Shakespeare, Racine and
other poets) together with her great critical qualities
and resourcefulness; all these were wonderful
standbys when there was no money and not much
else. Her inspiring company and vitality were a
great and much appreciated stimulus.

She provided me with dancers on whom to try my
faltering steps and was always there with her
enthusiasm and help. Those days at the Ballet Club

From Dame Alicia Markova

Alicia Markova as Marguerite in *Mephisto Waltz*.
[ASHTON]

I was asked to appear in the first programme of the new Ballet Club because Frederick Ashton wanted to stage *La Péri* for me. There was no money, of course, for anyone, and I remember Marie Rambert saying: 'Everyone is going to get 6s 6d a performance'. But eventually, because of circumstances, I landed up with 10s 6d: it was essential, since I needed a new pair of shoes for each Sunday night show, and these alone cost the 6s 6d. Then, because the curtain came down so late that I missed the last bus from Notting Hill to North Kensington where I then lived, I had to have a taxi, which cost 4s 0d. So I said that I really could not dance for less than 10s 6d–just to cover my expenses.

Those Sunday nights were wonderful, and they led to short seasons, still on the postage-stamp stage of the Mercury Theatre. In retrospect I realize that it must all have seemed rather odd for me, because with Diaghilev we had been used to the vast expanses of La Scala, Milan, or the Paris Opéra, or Covent Garden. Yet I never gave it a thought: we were all so busy and excited that there was no time or inclination to be grand or to make comparisons.

were very happy ones. Even when costumes seemed inadequate she would say, 'Don't worry, they will be lost in your beautiful movements.' Nevertheless, together with William Chappell, my life-long friend, and Sophie Fedorovitch, whom I met through Rambert and loved from the start for all her life, we did some successful things.

Today, Rambert's critical faculties are completely unimpaired, her eye is keen as ever and she can still put her finger on the weakness in any ballet, her humour endures and her heart throbs with deep humanity. My gratitude and enduring love, dear Mim, for our long-lasting and loving friendship.

With Frederick Ashton in *Mephisto Waltz*. [ASHTON]

How happy those Ballet Club appearances were for me! Marie Rambert was very important in my career: after Diaghilev's death, Ashton was the first person who wanted to work with me, and Rambert the second. She gave me somewhere to dance, and this was vitally important. I was among young people like myself, and they were enthusiastic. It wasn't simply the idea of becoming dancers that mattered to Rambert and her company, it was the idea of becoming *artists*. That is why, despite the huge difference I felt from my Diaghilev years, I was at home with the Ballet Club. Everyone thought seriously about choreography, designing, music: they were intent upon becoming true artists.

Alicia Markova as The Lady Friend in *Les Masques*. [ASHTON]

Pearl Argyle as La Fille au Bar, in *Bar aux Folies Bergère*.

From Dame Ninette de Valois

Are these reflections on the beginning of the 'Establishment' to end without any reference to the Mercury Theatre in Notting Hill Gate where the work of Dame Marie Rambert and Ashley Dukes encouraged the development of the English Ballet and the English drama all through the 1930s?

'The Ballet Club' was the foundation of today's Ballet Rambert, and the home of certain artists that did much to forward the general cause at Sadler's Wells when the theatre was able, by 1933, to offer a number of them a livelihood and further development of their talents.

Not that their work in Islington ever interfered with the valuable work in progress in their own theatre. They continued to appear there in the week-end performances and their free nights from the Wells. They continued under the above arrangement right up to the war, and the arrangement always proved itself to be a two-way flow of help, as the aims and the training of the Mercury dancers were the aims and training that we were instilling in the Sadler's Wells School, and much in preference to the average standard of the commercial theatre's professional dancers. Both companies joined forces for the Camargo Society performances.

Everybody loved the Mercury Theatre. In spite of its smallness its atmosphere for me was not far removed from that of the Festival Theatre, Cambridge, and the Abbey Theatre, Dublin. There was dedication; there was the love of the development of the theatre for itself; there was always a stream of dancers, actors and actresses ready to offer their services.

On the part of Dame Marie Rambert there was a devoted service given to the young artists that came her way, and Ashley Dukes–a distinguished author and critic–saw that his theatre served the young actors, actresses and dramatists of the day.

The work was executed on a miniature and very economical scale. Perfection was aimed at and often achieved in its various activities. Here was first seen a ballet that is still a major item in the more contemporary Ballet Rambert Company of today– Antony Tudor's moving *Dark Elegies*. At the beginning of the war there was staged, in a not very much larger theatre, Andrée Howard's one act gem *La Fête Etrange*. This is now in the repertoire of the Royal Ballet and the Scottish Ballet.

This little note of gratitude to the Mercury Theatre closes on one further comment. Frederick Ashton, the 'Petipa' of the English Ballet, did not come from Marseille but from Notting Hill Gate.

Eiizabeth Schooling and Walter Gore in *Bar aux Folies Bergère*   [DE VALOIS]

Antony Tudor, Maude Lloyd and Hugh Laing in *Alcina Suite*.   [HOWARD]

From Antony Tudor

Dearest Mim,

Fifty years a company – that is truly magnificent – and I suppose record shattering. How about that!

Isn't it lucky that you can take all the adulation in your stride – or else you would be all puffed up with pride and vanity and such like miserable deadly sins. But meantime, all of us humble disciples, being immature, can indulge them for any little parts we were favoured by the gods to play in this beautiful saga –

Love, Antony.

Lysistrata with left to right, Hugh Laing and Prudence Hyman, Walter Gore and Pearl Argyle, Antony Tudor and Diana Gould. [TUDOR]

Hugh Laing as The Mortal born under Mars in *The Planets*. [TUDOR]

Rambert Designs

Nigel Gosling

To single out any one facet of the Rambert pheno-menon can only be a limiting, indeed somewhat misleading operation. Her aims were always both high and comprehensive; her achievements thorough and well-rounded. Ballet for her was always part of a whole culture, indivisible, international, eternal. Her feeling for the present sprang from a faith that it was one with both the past and the future; she was interested in ballet as a whole, not as an *assemblage* of different arts.

She did not come into it late in life, as Diaghilev had, after earlier commitments to art and music. She came to it as a dancer and she saw stage designs as a part of the dancing experience; it is hard to imagine her agreeing to extreme experiments like, say, those by Picasso in *Parade*, in which the performers became animated stage props. She chose designs which would work on the stage and costumes which would help the dancers rather than those which would look pretty in the programme; and this is as true of the company today as it was fifty years ago.

In this sense it is impossible to do full justice in print to her choice, or to those of her successors. None of the designs look (as sometimes happens) better on paper than they did, or do, on stage, and some of them which hang vividly in the memory seem almost diffident in photographs or drawings. All the same, it is possible to pick out a few which convey the full Rambert flavour–a flavour which has shifted steadily with the changing years and yet retains, mysteriously, a character of its own.

This character was necessarily an expression of Rambert's own tastes, but it was also determined in part by the conditions of performance. The tiny Mercury theatre laid down strict terms of its own– Mozartian rather than Wagnerian, intimate rather than awe-inspiring. It was a place to set off private dreaming, not mass emotion. In the same way that the misplacing of a single finger could wreck the rendering of an ensemble, a false accent could undermine the whole stage picture. Poetry and drama had to be pursued with the stealth of an Indian; the mood of each piece, whether lyrical or sardonic, formal or romantic, hung each moment on a thread.

In this situation the audience itself became a big influence. In a theatre holding only 150 there was never any question of wooing a wide inexperienced public or competing with mass entertainment. Most of the spectators had recently dined on the riches of the Ballet Russes; what they looked for were high standards of performance and stylish presentation. This was an assembly of connoisseurs (and their friends) who looked for satisfaction, not for shocks.

The physical limitations of the stage were another prime consideration. The dance area was so small that even a single chair could prove an obstacle. The hanging of a cloth far enough forward to allow a dancer to cross the stage behind it would steal a valuable 2 feet, yet there was no room in the wings into which scenery could be slid. Apart from her dance-orientated approach and shortage of cash, one of the reasons why Rambert did not imitate Diaghilev and employ easel artists as designers except on rare and isolated occasions, was that in those days painting was almost exclusively a matter of pigment and canvas, and there was no room to reconstruct three-dimensional paintings on this tiny stage. Only the dancers, or a designer closely connected with their work, could cope with the conditions. This limitation is less severe today, when painters are accustomed to freer techniques; but the demands of the present company, with its taxing touring requirements, still operate in the same direction. Except in rare cases, the designs spring from a close knowledge of the character and conditions of the performances.

It is not surprising, then, to find that during the company's first years most of the designing was entrusted to a group of its own members–Susan Salaman, Hugh Laing, and above all, William Chappell and Andrée Howard. Salaman was used for her own ballets, which were charming but ephemeral; Chappell showed his mettle early with costumes for Ashton's *Capriol Suite* (1930) and went on to design many more of the Ashton ballets in which he was appearing himself–the start of a long and successful career as designer. Howard brought to her own designs exactly the same fluent economical, almost 'throwaway' deftness as she showed in the dances for which they were intended. Starting with *Our Lady's Juggler* in 1933, she went on to memorable work in *Mermaid* (the suggestion of a shipwreck by a few dancers and a tattered sail was a 'tour de force'), *Cinderella* (a miniature which encompassed the whole story), *Death and the Maiden*, with the victim tossed like a rag of chiffon by the

A Tragedy of Fashion: Elizabeth Vincent, Marie Rambert, Frederick Ashton, Frances James. [ASHTON]

Designs by Sophie Fedorovitch for dresses in *A Tragedy of Fashion*

John Armstrong's set design for the Camargo Society's production of *Façade* in 1931.
[ASHTON]

Nadia Benois' backcloth for *The Descent of Hebe*.   [TUDOR]

dark-cloaked attendants, the witty *Croquis de Mercure* and *Carnival of Animals*, and the touching *Sailor's Return*.

Predictably these designers worked very much from the dance outwards. The very first designs carried out for the company had revealed a stronger more positive approach, which a natural economy of style, surity of touch and sensitivity to the dance which marked them out as exceptional. *A Tragedy of Fashion* (1926) was not only the first Rambert ballet and the first Ashton ballet but the first ballet with designs by Sophie Fedorovitch–the start of a long collaboration both for the Rambert company and later for the Royal Ballet. Perhaps her most brilliant invention at the Mercury was her setting for *Les Masques* which translated the whole stage into a tiny night club with the little flight of steps which led into a dressing room serving as an elegant central feature of the sophisticated black and white set. Other outstandingly beautiful designs in her inimitable evocative style were for Ashton's *Mephisto Waltz* and *Valentine's Eve*.

Besides reconstructions of Bakst designs for Fokine ballets, several other outside designers contributed to those early years. The experienced George Sheringham devised some pastoral costumes for *The Lord of Burleigh* (1931); John Banting– one of the small band of British surrealist artists– designed *Adam and Eve*, Antony Tudor's ballet (with Tudor himself as the Serpent and Dolin as Adam with music by Constant Lambert); Nadia Benois, niece of Diaghilev's collaborator, introduced a strong Nordic flavour into her costumes and cloths for Tudor's *Dark Elegies* (she had already designed his *Descent of Hebe*, with amusing cut-out floor clouds to represent Olympus in the eighteenth century manner) and invented, later, a brilliant fox-woman costume for Mrs. Tebrick in Howard's *Lady into Fox*.

Another designer who worked extensively for Tudor was Hugh Stevenson, who devised some ingenious effects for his *Planets* (1934) and went on to create the tense twilight mood for his *Jardin aux Lilas* as well as the chastely sumptuous costumes and ballrooms for *Soirée Musicale* and *Gala Performance*. A dramatic change of mood was visible when Frank Staff took to choreography and mounted his *Peter and the Wolf* for which Guy Sheppard contributed a 'proto-Pop' setting which incorporated a flight of steps, a tin bath and a rubber duck.

After World War II the company changed its character considerably and undertook larger-scale ballets, including some of the nineteenth-century classics. Selections from these had often been part of the Mercury Theatre repertoire (the *Coppélia*

William Chappell: costume design for a gossip in *Lysistrata*. [TUDOR]

A
GOSSIP
IN
LYSISTRA

Hugh Stevenson: costumes for *Jardin aux Lilas*.　　[TUDOR]

extracts had been designed by the Russian Doboujinsky) and now such ballets as *La Sylphide* and *Don
Quixote* were addded to the repertoire; the designs
for such works were entirely suitable–Christopher
Ironside's *La Sylphide* sets were particularly attrac-
tive–but necessarily not of great originality.
Canterbury Prologue which unfortunately proved to
be short-lived had some vivid and distinguished
designs by the well known painter Edward Burra.

As was natural, a sharp change in design-style
occurred when the company acquired a new
Director, Norman Morrice, in 1966. From now on
modern dance rather than the classical *danse d'école*

was the dominating influence and a more promi-
nently contemporary note was struck in the decor
and costumes.

This change was continued under John Chesworth
and Christopher Bruce, for instance in the dramatic
setting, by Ralph Koltai and costumes, by Lindsay
Kemp, for Kemp and Bruce's *Cruel Garden*.

One of the features of today's designers is that
they prefer direct stage decoration to painted illu-
sion. The old painted cloths were jettisoned and
replaced by structures, lighting, and solid props,
while the costumes–often minimal, as modern
choreographers still prefer–become adornments for

Andrée Howard's design for Night in
Croquis de Mercure. [HOWARD]

Nadia Benois: costume design for *Lady into Fox*.
[HOWARD]

Andrée Howard: two costumes for *Carnival of the Animals*, The Hen and The Kangaroo. [HOWARD]

Edward Burra's set design for *Canterbury Prologue*. [PALTENGHI]

the body rather than indications of time, place or character. While several designers have contributed importantly to the company in this style, the most out standing is undoubtedly Nadine Baylis. Her designs often suggest sculpture, with shining elements of metal or perspex to pick up the elaborate lighting, while her costumes combine decoration and power. Recently, for Tetley's sea-girt *The Tempest*, she used yards of material in the same suggestive way.

Remote though this style–which continues under the present Director–may seem from that of the old Mercury Theatre, it perpetuates an approach which is both consistent and commendable. If such a thing as a typical Rambert design were to exist, it would be practical, memorable and cheap. That it would also be beautiful would be almost by the way; it would simply be part of a complete choreographic experience–an essential ingredient of the ballet, not a contribution to it. Rambert has always seen things whole.

Designs by M. Doboujinsky for the Mayor and Dr. Coppélius in *Coppélia*. [IVANOV]

Ralph Koltai's design for *Two Brothers*

Robin and Christopher Ironside: design for *La Sylphide*. [BOURNONVILLE]

Rouben Ter-Arutunian: costumes for *Pierrot Lunaire*. [TETLEY]

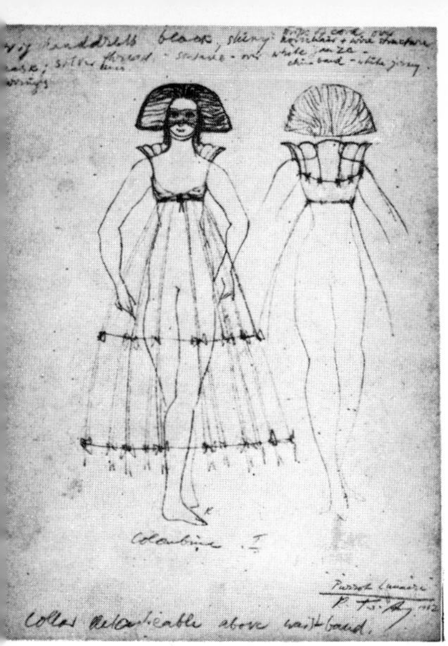
Colombine I
"Pierrot Lunaire"
Collar detachable above waistband.

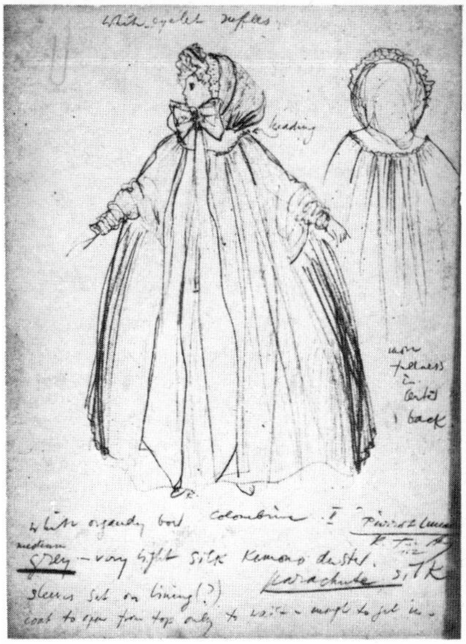
white eyelet ruffles
wadding
white organdy bow Colombine II "Pierrot Lunaire"
Grey - very light silk Kimono duster.
Parachute silk
sleeves set on lining(?)

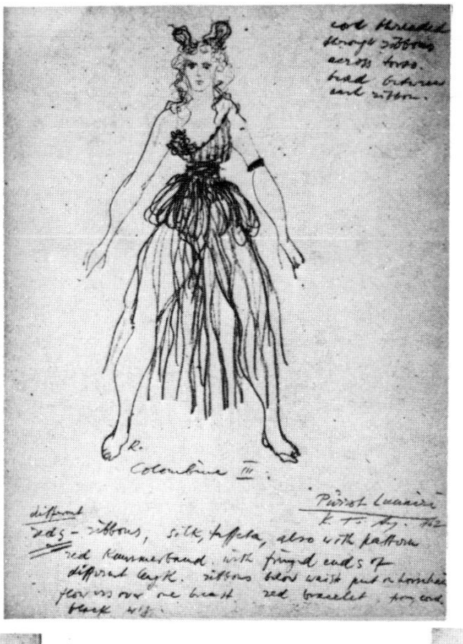
Colombine III
"Pierrot Lunaire"
different reds - ribbons, silk, taffeta, also with pattern
red Kummerband with fringed ends of different length.

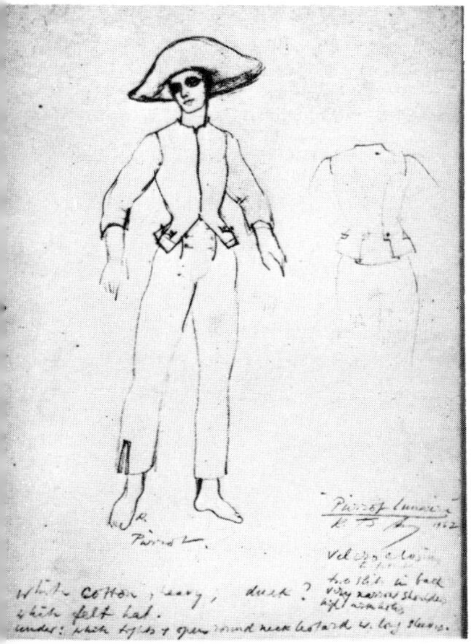
Pierrot
"Pierrot Lunaire"
white cotton, heavy, duck?
white felt hat.

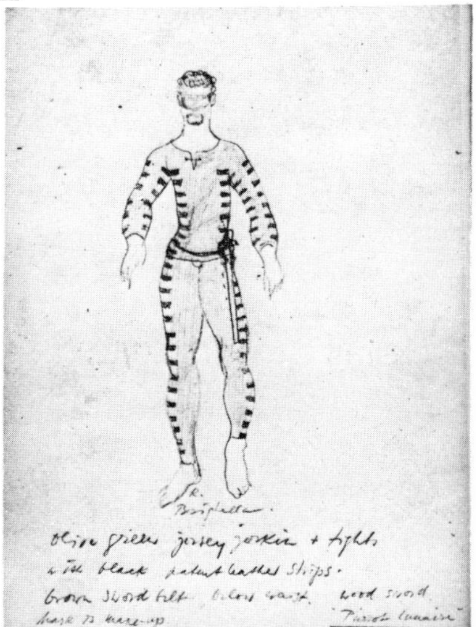
Brighella
Olive green jersey jerkin + tights
with black patent leather strips.
Brown sword belt below waist.
wood sword
"Pierrot Lunaire"

From Maude Lloyd

Maude Lloyd in *A Florentine Picture*.　　　　[ASHTON]

Already in 1925, five years before the Ballet Club
came into existence, the creative flow from the
Rambert studio had begun. I arrived from Cape
Town that year to continue my studies, and the first
modern choreography I saw was Ashton and Rambert herself appearing in *The Tragedy of Fashion* at the
Lyric Theatre at Hammersmith. Soon after that we
students all became involved in a production of
Spenser's *Faerie Queene* put on in London by the
O.U.D.S. with choreography by Ashton, the first
of the many works by Ashton in which I worked.

Both the Pavlova and the Diaghilev Ballets were
still in existence at that time, and we all went to as
many performances as we could afford, in the
gallery, of course. Rambert also used to take me to
Diaghilev performances and to visit the artists in
their dressing rooms. On the way home she would
talk of her time with the company when she was
working with Nijinsky. The Camargo Society
season gave us the experience of having many

modern works written for us – I remember learning
and dancing in *Job, The Origin of Design, The Lord of
Burleigh, High Yellow, Rio Grande, Façade*, besides
being in the 1932 production of *Giselle*, put on by
Sergueyev with Spessivtseva and Dolin in the
principal roles, and the white act of *Swan Lake*. That
same year we were immersed in the creation of the
Ballet Club.

All the new works there were geared to the tiny
stage, which tested the ingenuity of the designers
and the choreographers – to say nothing of the
dancers. I remember one evening standing at the
back of the stage, keeping as far back as possible

Sally Gilmour, Maude Lloyd and Celia Franca in *Les Sylphides*.　　　　　　　　[FOKINE]

behind the cloth, waiting for it to go up and reveal me. As it began to roll up, my skirt was caught up in it, and I stood higher and higher on point until somebody mercifully released me.

The principal girls' dressing room was a long narrow passage which led straight down onto the stage, and in order to gain the maximum space available designers often used the back wall and stairs up to the dressing room as part of their design. This meant that we sat there like chickens on a perch, trapped inside until the end of each ballet unless we escaped through the window onto the fire-escape! We moaned occasionally about the lack of elbow-room and Rambert, who shared the dressing room with us, used to silence us by telling an old Polish folk story about a peasant family who shared one room. Finding it impossible they asked advice from their village priest. To their astonishment he advised them to take in a goat as well. After a week they couldn't bear it and went back to him to complain. He told them to turn the goat into the yard. They did so, and their relief was so great that they never grumbled again. Mim was always a great

Hugh Laing and Maude Lloyd in *Valentine's Eve*.   [ASHTON]

optimist, in fact she used to find ways of persuading herself–and sometimes us–that unfortunate necessities, such as doing without a dancer or losing a piece of scenery, was actually an improvement. 'I really find it better that way,' she used to announce with suspicious conviction.

Being such a closely knit little group must, I think, have been a help to the choreographers; it certainly was to the dancers who were working with them. We always used to have our lunches together at the Express Dairy–decidedly modest meals.

Alicia Markova and Fred Ashton sometimes spent as much as 1s 3d on theirs: I usually survived on $10\frac{1}{2}$d. Antony Tudor, Hugh Laing and I spent our excess energy walking all over London, ending up quite often in the Bermondsey market; one day they bought two pathetic puppies in Petticoat Lane out of pity. The ups and downs in the health of these waifs became an important part of our lives. It was a real family existence where we all shared everything, good and bad, with Mim, with her driving vitality, at the centre.

From Diana Gould Menuhin

Dame Marie Rambert was my first teacher from the time I came to her at the age of nine till I left at nineteen. She gave herself utterly to her pupils, brain, body and soul, and if in that energy there was a fire that scorched many of us, I can never but be grateful for the fact that it was thanks to her training and from her studio that I was chosen (still a school-girl) by firstly Diaghilev and secondly Anna Pavlova.

Diana Gould.

Leda and the Swan: Diana Gould and Frederick Ashton in the centre. [ASHTON]

From Dame Peggy Van Praagh

Peggy van Praagh, *Dark Elegies* [TUDOR]

It was not until many years later that I realized how lucky I had been to be chosen by Marie Rambert to dance at her Ballet Club in the thirties. These were those exciting, wonderful years when the foundations of British Ballet were being laid.

In the first place I was lucky because I got in by the back door, not being a pupil of the Rambert School. I was a devoted student of Margaret Craske who entered me for the Advanced Cecchetti examination. This was a hard syllabus in those days, and Madame Rambert was one of my examiners. She had just lost three of her dancers to de Basil's Company, and offered me a position in her company as one of the replacements. That was in 1933.

We performed but once a week, on Sunday evenings, and only received expenses. In my case this was 2s 6d a week (just equal to my bus fares) but some dancers only received a shilling. So most of us were obliged to earn money elsewhere and thus did a variety of jobs. Luckily, I had several teaching commitments which I fitted in between rehearsals. Rehearsals took place at odd hours during the week, but mainly on Sundays. We arrived in the morning and worked feverishly all day until performance time.

These were chaotic, but exciting days. Madame Rambert, a ball of fire, was everywhere, sometimes screaming at us and someone, usually Hugh Laing, screaming back. There was often a lot of noise and frequently a crisis. But the show always went on.

The audiences were very distinguished. Only members of the Ballet Club could attend. These were often important people from the political, artistic and social worlds. (If we dancers were lucky we might meet some of those famous personalities after the show.)

The repertoire at that time was already very interesting and ballets that I especially loved were:

The Rape of The Lock: Joan Lendrum, John Andrewes, Pearl Argyle,
Frank Staff, Leslie Edwards and Peggy van Praagh whispering to Antony Tudor.   [HOWARD]

Foyer de Danse, Les Masques, Mephisto Valse and
Valentine's Eve – all choreographed by Frederick
Ashton. I was very proud to dance in these ballets.
But it was the Antony Tudor ballets, *Planets,*
Jardin aux Lilas and *Dark Elegies* that proved the
deepest experience and provided the chance for me
to create some roles of my own. The beautiful Pearl
Argyle was originally cast in *Jardin aux Lilas*, and
again my luck was in. She was by then also dancing
with the Vic-Wells Ballet and hadn't enough time
to rehearse, so her role came to me by default. How
the ballet was ever danced on the tiny Mercury stage
I cannot now imagine, but as so often with Rambert,
a miracle took place that night of 26 January 1936.
Possibly the closeness of the audience helped the
four of us (Maude Lloyd, Antony, Hugh and me) to
project an intensity of feeling and produce a mood

that brought, not only fantastic audience reaction,
but wonderful press notices.

From then on, not only the dancers, but the
public began to realize that Rambert had, in a few
years, produced two important choreographers,
Ashton and Tudor. They have continued to
influence ballet in this century, Ashton in the
United Kingdom and Tudor principally in the
United States of America.

A very memorable night for me was the premiere
of another Tudor masterpiece, *Dark Elegies* at the
Duchess Theatre, February 1937. This time the
press was unenthusiastic, but Rambert's belief
never wavered. Possibly this was her greatest asset.
She could be very critical of her artists, but her great
dedication and belief in what she was producing
remained steadfast and drove us all on to even
greater heights.

A Fragment from an Autobiography

William Chappell

However golden the haze blurring and burnishing the vistas of the past, we all have hundreds of small rooms tucked away in the back of the mind, full of dust and ghosts and whispers. All damp and gloomy as those church halls which acted as such unlikely incubators to the first progeny of the British Ballet.

I was a deeply involved art student of seventeen, when a friend, Lucy Norton, decided to introduce me to Marie Rambert, and I was bidden to take tea with a view to being considered as a pupil. Male dancers were at a premium in those days; and though Rambert had a dozen or so girl students her only

Rehearsal for *Leda and the Swan* at the Mercury Theatre in 1930. (Left to right) Pearl Argyle, Harold Turner, Andrée Howard, Frederick Ashton, Diana Gould, Prudence Hyman, William Chappell and Joan Benthall. [ASHTO

Mermaid: Pearl Argyle, William Chappell and Maude Lloyd.　　　　　　　　　　　[HOWARD/SALAMAN]

boy was Frederick Ashton.

I was amazed and rather bewildered by Rambert's small, bustling, volatile person; elegant in a rose beige jumper suit with a scarf at the neck held in place by a flower of the same crepe. Six inches taller and she would have epitomized those chic flat-chested, Eton-cropped women with a pearl at the lobe of each ear who filled the pages of Vogue. Her particularly bright dark eyes scanned me with a gaze piercing as a laser beam, probing my very vitals. She chattered ceaselessly; there seemed a pheno-menal outgiving of energy, an energy positively dynamic. Could it even be manic? I wondered, as she pulled at my arms, patted my shoulders, thum-ped me in the back. 'Lift the chin!' she ordered, pursing her lips and tilting her sleek head. 'Relax the shoulders! straighten the back, stretch the arms. Take an arabesque!' (What on *earth*, I thought, is that?) Standing on one leg in her drawing room with my toes turned in, I wobbled.

'Turn out the feet!' she cried; and snatching up a silver biscuit barrel she opened the lid revealing a few excessively dry water biscuits. 'Eat,' she said with relish as though offering some rare delicacy, 'Eat *plenty*!'

By the end of tea time, dazed, I found I had agreed to present myself at her studio a day or so later to be put through my paces at the 'barre' before she commenced her daily class at 10.00 am.

I was not altogether happy as on the appointed day, I approached the inevitable church hall. I think it was drizzling. It was always drizzling in the im-mediate vicinity of those church halls, however clear and dry it might be elsewhere; and there were always puddles on the paths leading to those grim Gothic doors opening on to windowless caverns, lit by glowing white electric bulbs; and giving out a wave of overpowering C of E perfume; a scent of dust and damp: mildew and mice. Finding myself unsuitably attired in baggy grey flannel trousers and a white shirt; attempting unsuccessfully, to point my feet in a pair of Mexican sandals; I decided almost immediately it was not my idea of what the ballet was about. (My ideas of what the ballet was about were the overwrought colours of *Cléopâtre*; the delicate charms of *Les Papillons*, and the Picasso decor for *Cuadro Flamenco*, all of which I had seen performed by the Diaghilev company when I was eleven years old. The ballet was also, and supremely, the darting iridescent figure of Pavlova; and the breathtaking glories of the Diaghilev-Bakst *Sleeping Princess*.) None of it had anything to do with stand-ing in this cheerless hall clutching a wooden rail, facing this eccentric little person who was now wearing a brief crepe-de-chine tunic and woollen tights, her small neat head made even neater by a bandeau of pink tulle; her snapping dark eyes pas-sionately intent on my every clumsy movement. Appraising: checking: taking a hundred mental notes, this concentration of interest was, and still is, a very typical characteristic of Rambert's. If some-thing, or someone, seems in any way worthy of her

'. . . elegant in rose-beige jumper suit
with a scarf at the neck . . .'

notice, she becomes immediately absorbed and
absorbing. One can almost hear the clicking and
ticking: the whirring and rustling of her restless and
curious mind.

My first lesson was brought to a conclusion by
the arrival of a half dozen or more young women,
swept in on a wave of fluting, lady-like voices, who
proceeded to disrobe on a dark staircase in the
corner. Exhorted by Rambert to return speedily for
more tuition, I could not get away fast enough, and
was greatly relieved to find myself once more in the
bustle of Notting Hill from whence I hurried to

Chelsea and the loving familiarity of my closed and
enchanted circle of art school friends.

It was quite some time before I returned to Rambert, and I think it must have been the invitation to
attend a matinée performance given at the Scala
Theatre by Rambert's students that prompted me to
try again. The girl dancers were appearing in a new
work *Les Nénuphars*, choreographed by one of
Mim's pupils, Frances James, with costumes designed by a painter Sophie Fedorovitch. She proved
to be yet another small, Eton-cropped person, but
one whose personality was the antithesis of Ram-

bert's, being quiet, calm and deliberate, with a low murmuring voice, and an eye just as observant and critical, only a little more mocking than Mim's. At first I found her a trifle forbidding: I grew not only to respect and admire, but also greatly to love Sophie.

The matinée included a divertissement with an item in which Frederick Ashton appeared as Harlequin. Unfortunately, during the performance he twisted an ankle and when I went back stage in company with my sister Honor (already at fifteen a West End chorine) we found Fred, a disconsolate figure sitting alone with his injured leg supported on a chair, still in his Harlequin costume and stage make-up.

We regarded with deep and grave interest his balletic *maquillage*. The matt and glowing skin: the exaggerated insect eyes: the curving polished garnet coloured lips. This, all this, was much more what I expected of the ballet. Perhaps I would, after all, go back to classes.

By the time I finally decided to become a ballet student Rambert had established her school in yet another church hall—one even more Gothic and certainly no warmer than the last. Here she remained; for here was to be the Mercury Theatre. The home of The Ballet Club and the breeding ground, the nest of the Ballet Rambert. Here over the next few years she began to draw together all the elements that were to form her company: and to reveal her true gift—her extraordinary capacity for uncovering and developing talent. As if she were some inspired and intuitive archaeologist, she would dig away at the layers of her students' minds and bodies until every atom of evidence of any latent talent was completely sifted and closely examined.

She combined these archaeological characteristics with the ways of a frantic mother bird, darting and hovering; flapping her wings; shrieking and chirruping over her brood. Admonishing; insulting; encouraging; persuading or demanding. Of course something had to come of it, and sure enough something did. Mim was not really a teacher. She was infinitely more complicated. She was, I would say, a very special kind of creator; a creator of creativity. At this particular time Fred was not much interested in the idea of becoming a choreographer. All his passion lay in trying to turn himself into one of the best male dancers in the world; and here it should be said, so I am saying it,

Fred was in fact a far better dancer than he was ever credited with being. His footwork was neat; he had a splendid bouncing jump, and unusual speed in movement, and without doubt the only real dancer's insteps in the company. However that may have been, Mim had other plans for him. She was I think determined to create a choreographer for her group. Eventually she created several, but this was the first. She began on her archaeological probing and daily, inexorably almost without his knowledge she drew out this new persona. Had it not been for her always enquiring mind, and her implacable eye, we might have waited much longer for him to reveal his gifts.

All dancers grumble. In truth, all performers of any kind, grumble. They always did and they always will. Even today when dancers are far more cossetted and cared for than they were in my day, they still grumble. During the burgeoning period (the early thirties) of Ballet Rambert we behaved as though we had been granted a special charter for grumbling. Were we not working ourselves (or so we thought) into the ground, for 3s 6d (boys) and 2s 6d (girls) per performance? We could hardly pay for our bus fares; let alone those extravagant one and threepenny luncheons at the local A.B.C. So we grumbled and muttered and moaned rebelliously among ourselves; and it never entered our heads that Rambert might be giving us a good deal more than those sad little pay packets. She was as it happened adding immeasurably to our artistic education; guiding our tastes musically and visually and bringing us into contact with every beneficial influence she could persuade toward us. Not every young dancer in those days was coached by the benign Goddess Karsavina or the spendid Woizikovski. Nor were they all visited as we were in our damp Gothic hall by the incomparable Pavlova and the incredible Diaghilev.

Pavlova arrived by mistake (and therefore unheralded) at the back door. Had those legendary high arched feet really picked their way through those ever present puddles on the pathway? Mim was in full cry, assuring us of our stupidity, lumpishness and general incompetence, as she put us through the movements of our only show piece, Fred's *Leda and the Swan* which we were to show to Madame. Our sudden paralysis and our transfixed faces made Mim abruptly aware of the presence—and **that, indeed, is what it was**—behind her. For a

(Tanqueray)

William Chappell
in
L'après midi d'un faune

moment panic and chaos reigned. Then the exquisite elegant figure floated forward and settled on a chair like one of the flowers or birds or elemental creatures she portrayed so perfectly.

Diaghilev came in by the right door. He sat like a grey stone Buddha, impassive and mostly silent. His basilisk Slav eyes flickered over us; and once or twice he inclined, almost imperceptibly, his large carved head towards Mim, and growled out a short comment in Russian. His expression never altered. I found him terrifying.

Apart from these, to me, positively mythical people we were constantly exposed to a stream of highly talented musicians. Constant Lambert, Jean Pougnet, Maria Korchinska, Eugene and Sidonie Goossens, Angus Morrison, Hugh Bradford and many more. We now began to receive a special stimulus from the type of audiences we were attracting to the Mercury Theatre and the Lyric,

Hammersmith. In those small theatres and particularly in the tiny Mercury we became very conscious of our public and, comprising as it did, a rare mixture of writers, painters, musicians, political economists, and the intellectuals of the *haut monde*, there must surely have risen some special emanation from so many lively minds, to which our young and impressionable persons could not fail to respond. It was not dull at The Ballet Club. Rambert had a vast ability to keep everything and everybody on the boil. Naturally we often boiled over. Backstage the air hummed like the swarming of bees. Tempers and temperaments inflated. Voices were raised. The boys behaved particularly badly: Harold Turner threw a chair at Fred because a role he expected had been given to Walter Gore. Walter would take offence at some criticism from Mim, leave rehearsal with a face of stone and vanish for days. Hugh Laing accused me of trying to ruin his appearance in a new ballet of Tudor's by designing a costume which failed to show his legs. We nearly came to blows. Tudor shouted at Mim. Fred shouted at Mim. I shouted at Mim and once threw a work basket at her. It was large and heavy: filled with cottons and buttons, needles, pins, scissors and other dangerous objects. Luckily it missed her. Andrée Howard and Mim's eldest daughter Angela were more or less permanently in floods of tears. Hugh Laing had a blazing row with Tudor just before a performance, climbed on to the roof in the pouring rain wearing nothing but a jock strap, and was only persuaded down just in time to get dressed and onto the stage. During one season at the Lyric, Hammersmith, at the end of a performance, a crowd of distinguished visitors were approaching the dressing rooms cooing and smiling, to be almost mown down by two howling, practically stark naked young men. Myself in front, pursued by Fred, his face contorted with fury, shouting abuse as he beat me about the shoulders with a knotted towel. I cannot remember what taunt I had offered to provoke this attack. The whole set up was crackling with vitality and therefore bound to explode periodically. No ill feeling lasted but quietly all the time, the solid foundations of several important international careers in the world of ballet were being established. Here were growing and developing the futures of Ashton; of Markova; of Pearl Argyle; Harold Turner and Antony Tudor; Andrée Howard and Sophie Fedorovitch.

William Chappell in *The Planets* with Pearl Argyle.

In its time and in its miniature way the company was a minor miracle. Rambert's influence in the ballet world during that extraordinary period when the deaths of Pavlova and Diaghilev had brought about the dissolution of both their companies, was incalculable. It was in fact, the moment, though at the time I do not think any of us realized it, when the balance of power began to move from the Russian, toward the Anglo-Saxon Ballet. During Rambert's close association with Nijinsky and Diaghilev she had absorbed into herself an essence compounded from the Parisian taste and elegance and the Slavic guts, passion, and colour which went to make up the potent mixture of the Ballet Russe. She took this essence and bathed each and everyone of us in it. The gifted ones absorbed it as she had done.

Line drawing by William Chappell.

Walter Gore on the stage of the Mercury Theatre
in the Sailor's dance from *Les Matelots*.

From Walter Gore

I never was completely lost in the embrace of Terpsi-
chore, probably because my upbringing was that of
an actor born of generations of actors, but it was
through Mercury I came to trust ballet and to
appreciate it, if not to be completely consumed by
the flame of its passion. Here it was I learned for all
time, so that it will remain as my shadow wherever I
go, the inestimable value of integrity.

By the same token it hasn't made for an easy life,
where one is perpetually scrupled between the
pincers of necessity, but from this theatre of 150
yellow velvet seats came all that was best in ballet.
Discipline, adventurous progress, respect for
tradition, life in art, high purpose, and a true
realization of what was expected of us. And fun.
The honest spirit of those days is now a war away,
but praise be I was in time. I feel sorry for those who
never knew ballet before it became a victim of Mass
Crass Production, with its attendant lazy Wurlitzer
mentality. I feel sorry they never knew the staccato
rush of taffeta down Shooting-stick Alley.

Nostalgic thoughts? If you believe they are
nothing more than that it is clear you never knew
the real Mercury, or what changed it from a Non-
Conformist Church Hall into a powerhouse for
ballet. Had only the magic trick of that transforma-
tion not been lost all would yet be well.

This is no nostalgia: no clamouring for the past
as a glass-enclosed mantelpiece souvenir, but for
what that past had to show for itself. We were not
then, as I remember, anything but unconscious
Livingstones discovering our own Zambesis and
Victoria Falls with equally excited hearts. Rightly so
I believe. We were unhappy at times certainly – who
isn't, even under perfect conditions – but over it all
rose in strong battle array our beliefs in ourselves
and our futures. We were prepared and ready to take
our places eager-eyed and youthful, not with
jealous pride but with zealous pride.

It is very salutary to remember how much was
achieved willingly, or in my case unwillingly, on
6s 6d a Sunday performance, when ballet in London
was the cherished property of the now dispersed,
dispossessed and despised 'Elite': and to remember
the day when ballet in the provinces wasn't worth a

Walter Gore in *Simple Symphony*.   [GORE]

sack of waterlogged rice. Yet despite all the hazards, though I prefer to think it was because of their obstinate existence, we achieved what had never been before: English ballet as a hall-mark in the real sense of the word.

This is why a livelier pen than mine, should write at length so that all may know of the life and times, grave and brave, of those Angels on a Pin's Head *and* of the Pin on which span they balanced: but let it not be as a Dusty Discourse on Dates. The dates in themselves are unimportant: it is the breathing of the years which matters.

Had the Mercury not existed, and let us by no means forget The Squire of Notting Hill* in this respect, ballet in England would have been so very much slower in blossoming and might very well have taken a very different course, and certainly we would never have known those impromptu 'after performance' performances by Ashton, Chappell, Bartolin, Howard, and with Hugh Bradford at the piano.

The roots set down there so long ago in that Non-Conformist Church Hall have spread throughout the world and the gilded figure of Mercury still hovers over that slate roof where one used to lie in the sun when there was any. Unofficially, of course.

No matter what he, or you Madame, think of the New Order under his winged feet, Madame – Mother Ballet of England – I salute you from afar, and with memories of Dymchurch and cold grey tumbling seas, I wish you many a wonderful evening among your so many acolytes and friends. With love from Wally – so hopeless yet so hopeful, as you once wrote.

Andrée Howard and Elizabeth Schooling as the ugly sisters in
Cinderella with Walter Gore as the hairdresser.   [HOWARD]

Walter Gore as *Mr. Punch*.
[GORE]

From **P. W. Manchester**

Like most people who were in close contact with Rambert over an extended period, I feel I learned more from her than anyone I ever knew. Not that she consciously set out to educate (or did she, at least some of the time?) but it simply was not possible to remain unignited from the sparks ceaselessly emanating from that ever-active mind.

Not that she couldn't put you into embarrassing positions, mainly due to her own total un-self-consciousness. One of my most vivid memories of the time in which I acted as her secretary and a sort of assistant company manager during World War II, is when I happened to quote, rather aptly in the circumstances, a couple of lines from a Shakespeare sonnet. Mim recognized Shakespeare immediately, duly relished it, but was a little surprised that the sonnet was not among the many she knew by heart.

A few minutes later we were both on a bus on our way to the Arts Council. The moment we sat down Mim commanded: 'Bill, tell me the whole of the sonnet'. Have you ever tried recollecting a poem you hadn't given much thought to for years and had certainly never expected to recite aloud – and on a bus, yet? I tried to mumble my way through it, only to be ordered to 'speak louder, I can't hear'. Mercifully at that point Mim became impatient with the bus's imperceptible rate of progress and leapt to her feet, off the bus and into a passing cab, with me trailing in her wake. I was able to finish the sonnet in the privacy of the cab and we never referred to it again. But she probably had it by heart before she went to sleep that night.

I have another memory of her which I dearly cherish. One evening in Bedford during a company tour, Mim came scurrying gleefully into the theatre. At that time she was in the habit of wrapping herself into a singularly voluminous long grey cloak out of which only her bright eyes and imperious little nose were visible. As she was hurrying along, a man stopped for a moment and said: 'Oh, you dear little mouse'. Mim loved that.

Mouse she may have looked; but all who over the years have had the privilege of being a friend and colleague know that she is a lion in heart, mind and soul.

Marie Rambert taking a curtain call with Sally Gilmour (Giselle) Walter Gore (Albrecht), Joyce Graeme (Myrtha).

From Sally Gilmour

I was twelve years old when I went as a student to Marie Rambert, so that I feel I grew up with her. Our morning classes were taken by Antony Tudor, and in the afternoons by Rambert, always elegant, very dynamic, a rather glamorous figure. These classes were always exciting, and there were also the Sunday night performances at The Ballet Club which were so wonderful, with Ashton's, Tudor's and Andrée Howard's ballets–a dream-like world of incredible and brilliant people.

Once I had been accepted into the company, and especially during the war years when several of us lived with Rambert, I became very close to her. She was completely part of the company, always working with us while she gave classes and always in front or standing in the wings during performances. Afterwards she gave copious notes and discussed the performance, not only your performance but everyone's, so you were conscious of the ballet as a whole and everyone's part in it, and also your own progress. There was a constant challenge of her wanting us to do better and better. It was typical of her that I remember her saying 'We have a new girl coming. She has no neck, but she has a wonderful quality, and I will get that extra 2 inches of neck out of her'. And she did. This was her unique approach; not to dismiss anyone because of their shape but to recognize what they had to give and develop that quality. During the war years we performed for CEMA, and the constant work with no holidays, the discomforts and stimulation of playing to so many different people (many seeing ballet for the first time) often doing weeks of one night stands, made the company into a family, or so it seemed to me.

Rambert was infinitely aware of the spirit of a ballet and meticulous that you did not change that spirit or a single step. If there was anything anyone did which was 'less than required' she pounced on it at once. She made us understudy and learn everyone's part, and would never let us rest on what we had achieved. I could never have left Rambert if I hadn't married. She wanted the best she could get out of you, *for you*, and would go to any lengths to get it. I grew up with her as a dancer, and a person, and still feel very very close to her.

Sally Gilmour and Andrée Howard at a costume fitting for *The Sailor's Return*. [HOWARD]

Sally Gilmour as Tulip in
The Sailor's Return.
[HOWARD]

Lady into Fox: Charles Boyd and Sally Gilmour. [HOWARD]

Lady into Fox: Sally Gilmour. [HOWARD]

Changing the form, preserving the tradition

NORMAN MORRICE
talks to Peter Williams

It's twenty-one years since you first joined Ballet Rambert?

Amazingly yes! It's hard to imagine how the time passed so quickly–first as a raw recruit, then as a soloist dancer, choreographer, and finally for the past eight years during which Madame allowed me to run the company with her and to make the changes which I felt were very necessary for the time. It was marvellous that she had the desire to let the company change, something that's been happening all her life I think. I always thought of her as Madame, or just plain Rambert; she always called me, and still does, Morrice. At the time I joined there was already a Norman in the company.

You did in fact become one of Rambert's most important choreographers after that first generation mainly stemming from the original Ballet Club. When did you first become interested in this?

I was probably more interested in choreography than in dancing right from the beginning. It was seeing the Tudor works in the repertory, long before I even dreamed of becoming a dancer, that interested me most of all. But it became obvious that I would have to become a dancer in order to understand how to become a choreographer. It was almost a lucky chance that I became one, since a choreographer didn't turn up for a Rambert season and Madame, whom I think knew instinctively from school days that I was interested, decided to give me the chance. You yourself were in at the inception of that first work. Madame gave me the company and three days; then said she would look at what I had done and at the same time she brought in a group of people, of which you were one, and I have never been so scared in all my life. I had done roughly ten minutes of what was to become my first ballet, *Two Brothers*.

Your relationship with Madame has been a rather unique one?

Yes. We got to a marvellous moment when we could disagree. Often Rambert would say 'Don't say "yes" when you don't mean it!'; on occasions we would scream at each other. I remember one alarming occasion at the Jeannetta Cochrane Theatre when Madame, from the top of the stairs and I, from the bottom of the stairs, were yelling our disagreements at each other. My secretary was trapped in between us and promptly burst into tears. Immediately, Madame and I completely forgot what our argument was about in our concern for this poor girl. Against all this, however, Madame taught me so many things about dance and art, about attitudes to work and through that, probably, a lot about life.

We would often go into Holland Park and there were many occasions when I would sit freezing on a bench beside her, she never seemed to get cold, but her passion–about a particular tree, or a squirrel or bird or a child–was quite extraordinary and became poetic. So much so, in fact, that I never really felt

Lucy Burge and Joseph Scoglio in *There was a Time*.

Two Brothers: Gillian Martlew and John Chesworth. [MORRICE]

1-2-3: Mary Willis, Christopher Bruce, Peter Curtis. [MORRICE]

the cold. She would suddenly speak about Shakespeare, quote endlessly, and try to trap me into saying where it all came from, of course I never knew! But I learned so many things and it was from our private conversations – about performances within the company, the progress of certain dancers, the attitude of the dancer to rehearsal, from her extraordinary recognition of talent – that helped me enormously when I had to start taking control of the company. I'll never forget it.

Madame is such a mixture of so many things, she can be incredibly kind then sometimes rather cruel. I feel the cruelty was often something to do with frustration because she couldn't get one to work fast enough or long enough and was always longing to see the potential achieved. There is another side to her – a wonderful sense of humour. She has this great fund of jokes, some of them very dubious such as the one about 'the young lady of Gloucester . . .'; where she got them from I just cannot imagine. They always corpsed me but it irritated me that I could never remember them myself.

When was it that you felt that Ballet Rambert should change its form? I hesitate to use the word 'image' since I know it is a word that Rambert detests!

The feeling began shortly after we made *Don Quixote* in 1962. I felt at the time that the company was becoming too classically orientated, anyway for my taste. There were several other companies in the country also doing the classics and they had enough money to do them on a lavish scale; it seemed to me that Ballet Rambert had become less and less creative in terms of new work and in developing new choreographers. At the time it hit me that the direction in which we were going might not be the right one, but I was then only an employee and was certainly in no position to change the company's policy. A few years later, however, the company found itself in the middle of a financial crisis and it was obvious that something had to be done. It was then that I was asked whether I could produce some kind of plan that might save the issue.

The plan really proved to be a return to the early days of Rambert. The idea was to get back to it being a choreographers' company that would make its own repertory. The constant touring with the classical company had made it quite impossible for us to find enough creative time. I felt that with our classical background we should extend our possibilities movement-wise by bringing in choreographers from America and seriously to study a modern technique; if we could work on both techniques we could make a transition into what's known as modern dance, much quicker. It was a case of asking those in the old company, who might have an interest in the change, whether they would be prepared to risk it and, sadly, let the others go. It's never easy but, with the agreement of Madame and with the co-operation of the Arts Council, we were given three months' grace to produce a new company.

For two years it was very hard because we were not quite sure what we were aiming for; it was a case of making an environment in which one hoped a new creative thrust would emerge. Eventually it did and within five years we had a totally new repertory, much of it by choreographers from within the company and some marvellous additions from masters from abroad. One of the important things from our point of view was to have an American choreographer, Glen Tetley, come to create a new work on the company and his *Ziggurat* was our first new-wave ballet in that it changed our ideas about setting (he used Nadine Baylis), about lighting, about the shape of choreography and music. For us it was a totally new experience and although working with him is extremely demanding it certainly helped to increase our stamina. With all these new experiences the company gradually began to move in a way in which you couldn't see the seam between classical and modern techniques. So with that we produced, I hope, a new type of movement and, with visitors from abroad, inspiration for our own people to make new works and consequently a new repertory.

We also found that, whereas in the past we had been a rather isolated company, we were getting used to people watching us; we started a new thing of allowing sculptors, designers, photographers and even ordinary visitors, to come and watch us doing class and rehearsing and creating. This led us into having a collaboration with the Central School of Art and Design in which we put our novice choreographers together with young students of design; we gave them a week of performances so that they could see their ballets and judge how they were getting on. We had panels, which were sometimes chaired by yourself, in which the works

Freefall: Jonathan Taylor and Mary Willis. [TETLEY]

Embrace Tiger and Return to Mountain. [TETLEY]

Ziggurat: Norio Yoshida, Nelson Fernandez, Michael Ho and Stephen Ward, with Yair Vardi, seated, as the God. [TETLEY]

could be discussed and the ideas thrown around. This began a new process and the dancer became less isolated from the rest of the world and that was very good.

So by the time you left, after eight years, you had really formed the foundation of a new type of dance company, certainly as far as Britain is concerned?

I like to think so. I liked what happened and I felt that something had been achieved which boded well for the future. Most exciting of all was that I think British choreographers were being born again after a long period in which there was so little creative activity. I am sure that the company will change again and again but I hope that there will always be a nucleus of really creative people who are prepared to work hard, to take risks and to carry on those traditions which Madame inspired fifty years ago.

The destination is the same

John Chesworth

John Chesworth rehearsing with Sandra Craig.

Forecasting the future is usually best left to professional star gazers, or to members of the crystal ball brigade. Still, one is not so naive as to imagine that pure chance or accident will suffice to form a forward looking artistic policy. Planning and direction are needed even if practical considerations are sometimes put aside to allow one to indulge in the luxury of dreams and ambitions.

Faced with the task of looking ahead I took as my starting point, the Ballet Rambert in 1976, its fiftieth anniversary year, but that word anniversary redirected the focus of my thoughts, and instant nostalgia triumphed – I was looking back in time.

My own working memories of the company only cover the last twenty-five years, but recently I was looking through some old photographs which had been collected together for an exhibition. Quite a number of them I had never seen before, but in so many, particularly those taken in rehearsal, one was aware of something beyond just the frozen image caught by a camera. Looking carefully at the faces one could detect in the eyes expressions of both hope and determination, qualities necessary in

facing the great challenge that lay ahead of them. Would that we could turn the clock back to those days, and question them about their thoughts for the future. However, actions speak louder than words, and I think they made their point by the achievements that emerged from that cradle of British ballet. We of today's company are very aware of the debt we owe to those early pioneers, and to all of those who followed them and contributed their talents towards keeping the company alive, thus enabling us to continue the tradition of constant re-assessment, discovery and creation.

When I took over from Norman Morrice I was asked if there would be any radical changes in artistic policy. Immediately an image came to mind, corny perhaps but still very apt. My reply was 'The destination is the same, but en route we may have different ports of call'. I would like to think that this so called destination is in the furthest galaxy, intangible. For those who have been lucky enough to scale the ultimate heights, and conquer Everest, where do they go from there? Only down.

It is rather incongruous but our future is summed

up by our past. Faces change, fashions change, styles change, but an ideal as inspiring as the one that has always been the strength of the Rambert company lives on as long as honesty, dedication and artistic integrity remain.

Throughout the years since 1926 the image of Ballet Rambert has always been associated with a group who were contemporary to the times. It has never stood still and marked time, for always within it there have been imaginative minds, not afraid to express themselves by taking risks, and challenging the then accepted artistic fashions. This is our heritage from the past, and we are proud to carry it forward into the future, Arts Council willing!

Unfortunately finance is a controlling factor in any future planning, and to keep up the highest professional level of presentation in conjunction with a large creative output on a very tight budget, all this costs us more than mere money for it puts an enormous strain on all the dancers and staff; in fact our turnover of personnel is not usually caused by disillusion, but simply by people becoming burnt out. The success of the company is almost literally achieved by the lucky survivors standing on the bodies of those who have fallen. Will the future change all this? I doubt it, for art is a very demanding master possessing very little sense of compassion or pity.

So how do we face the future? Still with the conviction that our main purpose is to provide an atmosphere where creation can take place. An atmosphere in which talent can be discovered and encouraged to flourish, whether it be from a dancer, choreographer, designer, composer or lighting designer. Constantly we will be working towards extending our performing range, which so far has encompassed workshops, lecture demonstrations, children's programmes, thrust-stage projects, all of them extras to the normal repertoire theatre performances. Still hardly explored are the creative possibilities presented by television, video, film and collaborations with actors and singers.

To support these creators we have a dedicated group of people concerned with administration, music, publicity and the staging of the finished work, which is then presented throughout this country and abroad to an ever increasing audience, of which a large percentage are in the younger age group.

Our weapons consist of sheer guts, imagination and the conviction that we are treading the right path. To these we can add the greatest prize of all, in the outstanding example of Madame Rambert's fifty years of selfless struggle in which she demonstrated such courage and provided such inspiration to others. I am proud to be entrusted with the inner burning light of her convictions with which to attempt to see through the darkness ahead.

Bertram Batell. Ballet Rambert children's sh

John Chesworth,
Marie Rambert and Norman Mor

Time Base: Sandra Craig and Peter Curtis, Marilyn Williams and Dreas Reyneke.　　[CHESWORTH]

Wings: Susan Cooper, Julia Blaikie, Marilyn Williams, Nicoline Nystrom and Sandra Craig.　　[BRUCE]

Running Figures: Lenny Westerdijk and Zoltan Imre. [NORTH]

Ricercare: Leigh Warren and Lenny Westerdijk. [TETLEY]

Towards new horizons

Peter Williams

Creativity is the word that will always immediately spring to mind in anything to do with Marie Rambert's adventures in dance. It must be admitted though that towards the end of her company's first forty years, creative ideas were wearing thin although there were admirable medium-scale versions of some of the standard classics. It became obvious that a shot-in-the-arm was needed if the ideals and traditions, that made Ballet Rambert unique in the world of dance, were to be upheld.

The necessary shot came when Norman Morrice was appointed co-artistic director with Marie Rambert in 1966. Morrice, a dancer and choreographer who had grown up in the school and company, had spent some time in America studying modern dance forms mainly with Martha Graham; he was also influenced by the integration of classical and contemporary forms in the work of Netherlands Dance Theatre. It was his decision to change Ballet Rambert into something more compact and with a policy similar to that of the Dutch company.

The change-over process was to take a few years before the company re-established its own identity but the main factor in bringing this about was the introduction of works by American choreographer, Glen Tetley. 1967 saw no less than four Tetley works brought into the repertory - two revivals, *Pierrot Lunaire* (which established Christopher Bruce as a major artist) and *Ricercare*; two creations, *Freefall* and *Ziggurat*. There is not the slightest doubt that Tetley was to influence a whole new generation of emerging choreographers. That new choreographers were being given the opportunity to develop came with the inauguration, in 1967, of workshop programmes which had public performances.

These 'Collaboration' programmes, which have continued intermittently, involved choreographers with composers and young designers, mainly from the Central School of Art and Design; they were given during the early years at the School's own Jeannetta Cochrane Theatre though in more recent years workshop programmes took place at Riverside Studios. In the early 1970s the company's work was further extended into the field of education with productions such as *Bertram Batell's Sideshow*

and, in 1975, *Take a Running Jump* primarily intended for children; these and many similar educational programmes, some with the aim of explaining works in the current repertory, have played a great part in the success the company now enjoys.

After 1971, Tetley's association with the company became more tenuous, although he returned from time to time to create very notable works, but he left an indelible mark upon the company's reshaping, especially on its choreographic image. Through this, many of the established and emergent choreographers found a new though entirely personal identity which became apparent in Morrice's *That is the Show* (1971). Then Christopher Bruce developed into a major choreographer through a number of works, outstanding being his ... *for these who die as cattle* (created for the open stage at the Young Vic in a 'Dance for New Dimensions' programme in 1972), *Ancient Voices of Children* (1975) and *Black Angels* (1976). In addition to works created by company members - such as John Chesworth, Jonathan Taylor, Joe Scoglio, Gideon Avrahami - the 1970s also saw valuable contributions from distinguished American contemporary choreographers such as: Anna Sokolow, Louis Falco, Lar Lubovitch, Manuel Alum, Cliff Keuter.

For eight years, Norman Morrice had shouldered the entire responsibility of reshaping Ballet Rambert and he felt that the company had now reached a state that it could carry on; in 1974 he left to work as a freelance choreographer with various foreign companies, later returning to England as artistic director of the Covent Garden Royal Ballet. Morrice's successor with Rambert was John Chesworth, with Christopher Bruce as associate director and choreographer. By this time the policy had become firmly established and things continued in much the same way except that the Chesworth/Bruce period produced something entirely new to the Rambert repertory - two full-evening contemporary dance works. The idea may have been engendered by the fact that in 1971, London Contemporary Dance Theatre put on a full-evening work produced by Robert Cohan; his multi-media *Stages* had been largely responsible for bringing a whole

Pierrot Lunaire: Christopher Bruce as Pierrot; Gayrie MacSween as Columbine; Jonathan Taylor as Brighella. [TETLEY]

new and younger generation to dance. It was in 1977 that mime artist Lindsay Kemp, with Bruce as choreographer, devised for Rambert a spectacle - involving dance, mime, song and speech - based on the life and tragedy of the Spanish poet, Federico Garcia Lorca. This work, *Cruel Garden*, in a mixture of realism and poetic fantasy, reflected Garcia Lorca's reaction to aspects of life in his native Spain, then on the brink of civil war, and to the oppression he found on a visit to America. It was a work of great theatrical power which has continued to have great box-office appeal in Britain as well as on the company's foreign tours. In 1979, Glen Tetley returned to create a full-evening work based on Shakespeare's *The Tempest*. Arne Nordheim's score and Nadine Baylis's designs combined with Tetley's choreography in a work of magical beauty which focused more on the symbolic essence of Shakespeare's play rather than being a descriptive narrative, although the play's characters and many of the incidents were most skilfully woven into the texture of the piece. The success of the work was helped enormously by the fact that the company gave an explanatory schools programme, *Inside The Tempest*.

Finale of *Betram Batell's Sideshow*

More changes of direction when Chesworth and Bruce left in 1980, although the latter remained as associate choreographer. The new resident choreographer was Richard Alston who had been one of the original dancers in London Contemporary Dance Theatre, also one of its most promising young choreographers. Since his Rambert appointment, Alston has created *Landscape* and *Rainbow Ripples* in 1980; in 1981 he created a new version of Stravinsky's *The Rite of Spring*. Even though for nearly a year the company had no artistic director as such, and was run by a consortium, the policy never faltered; the dancing standards remained consistently on an even higher level, due in a great degree to the work of the ballet mistress, Sally Garbutt. By April '81, Robert North, formerly a distinguished dancer and choreographer with LCDT, took over the directorship. A new phase opened up for the company which Marie Rambert started some 55 years ago; through all the changes it has been her indomitable spirit, her continued unflagging enthusiasm, that has been the driving force behind this unique contribution to dance in Britain.

That is the Show: Gideon Avrahami, Christopher Bruce, Joseph Scoglio, Jonathan Taylor.   [MORRICE]

Ancient Voices of Children: Lenny Westerdijk, Sally Owen, Sylvia Yamada. [BRUCE]

Black Angels: Michael Ho, Diane Walker, Lucy Burge, Catherine Becque, Guy Detot, and, in the foreground, Paul Melis. [BRUCE]

Cruel Garden: John Tsakiris as the Bull and Christopher Bruce as the Poet. [BRUCE/KEMP]

The Puppet Scene from *Cruel Garden*.

The final scene from *Cruel Garden*.

Robert North in his ballet
Lonely Town, Lonely Street.

Richard Alston.

Rainbow Ripples: Catherine Becque,
Rebecca Ham, Cathrine Price,
Guy Detot and
Nelson Fernandez. [ALSTON]

The Rite of Spring: Catherine Becque,
Sally Owen, Quincy Sacks, Rebecca Ham,
Diane Walker and Cathrine Price as the
Adolescents and Yair Vardi as the Sage.
[ALSTON]

Prospero's island

GLEN TETLEY
talks to Peter Williams

How was it that you came to make a ballet on The Tempest?

When I was with the Stuttgart Ballet a very wonderful man, Herr Grub, who was head of the Schwetzingen Festival came to me and said he would like to commission me to create a full-evening work. I said I had never done one but that I would certainly think about it. At that time I had been working with Arne Nordheim on *Greening* for the Stuttgart Ballet and, for a full-evening theme, I had been thinking about various Shakespeare plays. The one that has always intrigued me most was *The Tempest*. So I suggested this and said that I thought Nordheim would be the ideal composer. This was four years ago, and then I was thinking of it in terms of a large company like the Stuttgart company. But then

again, it is a very intimate play and I couldn't see the play in terms of the classical vocabulary, like putting people on point and all the things one would need to do with a big classical company.

Then I found myself not in Stuttgart, and Herr Grub came and told me that the commission remained with me wherever I wanted to go. I started to think about the enormity of this whole project and felt the only company where I could have the peace and quiet and a long rehearsal period would be a company like Ballet Rambert. I approached them, and they were very excited and said they would clear three months, which I considered to be minimal rehearsal period, out of their performing schedule to give me this time in London and that they would take care of the whole organisational part.

So, thinking in terms of a smaller company and of doing *The Tempest* in a more contemporary language, for me the Rambert has been ideal. There are only 20 dancers, and in a strange way it has increased the metaphorical part of *The Tempest*

The Tempest: Thomas Yang as Caliban, Gianfranco Paoluzi as Ariel. [TETLEY]

because not only are these same dancers the principal characters but they must in turn become all of those other people such as spirits, nymphs, mermaids and so on.

Although Shakespeare's The Tempest *has some of the most beautiful poetry in the language it doesn't immediately strike one as an ideal subject for a dance work. Why did you choose it?*

Although there is not a great deal of narrative in the play, the action and the characters are symbolic and this appeals to me. As I see it, the whole idea of the play is something that is happening in Prospero himself; he is the tempest, the turmoil. When thinking of *The Tempest* in terms of dance, it has in its favour the fact that it has more of a masque element, more dance/song than in any other Shakespeare play; it has so many characters whose very nature is of dance itself.

How did you work with Arne Nordheim? Did you explain your concept of the play or did he write the score and then you worked from that?

Well, I have a great love for Arne as a person and a great love and respect for his music. He's a 20th-century composer who is fascinated with every aspect of sound. Like me, he also has a great love of nature, he loves sounds in nature and the frequencies that happen in nature: wind sounds, water sounds, animal sounds, bird sounds. It seemed to me that Nordheim was the logical composer for *The Tempest* as I wanted to do it.

It was $3\frac{1}{2}$ years ago that he came to me, during the holiday season, in Italy and worked with me for two weeks. Every day we took the play apart, scene by scene and speech by speech. As we did so we saw this very musical construction of it. Shortly after that, when we had prepared a whole graph of the play, I saw a production of *The Tempest* which was an eye-opener to me because it seemed to lack every kind of visual excitement that a production could lack. I was so disappointed that I rang Nordheim and told him there was no way in which we could paraphrase the play, it was absolutely the wrong way of going about it. So I told him to write a very strong piece of music with a very strong musical form and then I could write a very strong choreographical form. I knew that Petipa gave very precise instruction to Tchaikovsky when they were working on *The Sleeping Beauty*; it was almost like a railroad timetable, breaking every-thing down to eight measures of this, 16 and 32 measures of that and so on. But I had already decided that I only wanted two acts because, with

a concentrated play like *The Tempest*, I didn't want to break it up with long intervals. Having made that break, and considering that the first act was exposition of all of this material and the second act was resolution of it, and trying in some way to respect the classic tenets that Shakespeare adopted for the play, Nordheim then began working on the score from a musical standpoint.

The process hasn't been one that meant that everything sprang from our heads just together, the material is too massive. It's been a slow-working process and it's been amazing, working over a three-year period, how many other elements have gone into *The Tempest* so that it has arrived in the form we have now evolved. We discussed the question of those incredible speeches and we both decided that there should be two singers, as I wanted the original songs in it; these and some of the key speeches occur in the musical setting so there is that tie-in with the play itself. For instance, Caliban's beautiful speech '. . . Be not afeard. The isle is full of noises, and a thousand twangling instruments . . .', that has been a very key element of the first act. Also his cry for freedom which is a cry all through the play from everyone who is trying to find freedom in some way or another.

It was about two years ago in New York that, while going into Leonardo da Vinci's notebooks, I suddenly realised that Leonardo was a Prospero: in his thinking, in his magic books, in his diagrams, the period he was in Milan, his exile, the trouble with his servants. But Leonardo has entered into this work in very strange ways, because the very first piece of music that Arne wrote is based on Leonardo's wheels; there are cycles of thematic material melody which occur in 30 second intervals, within that 15 seconds, within that $7\frac{1}{2}$ seconds, so forming a wheel within a wheel. It's a beautiful section of music which opens and closes the ballet and is not unlike the sea itself.

I am very sensitive to music and cannot respond to music I cannot choreograph. So knowing the play and having read it over and over again, it was a question, when I got the first act of the music, of finding a form that fitted in with the play and what the music said. That's an endless procedure, because when it came to the Rambert dancers there came another element, in that I had to relate the movement quality to, say, Lucy Burge as Miranda, Christopher Bruce as Prospero and so on. It's been an endless, and wonderful, three-dimensional, twelve-sided crossword puzzle.

How literal a translation of the play is your ballet?
It would be ridiculous to do a paraphrase of the play without the words. But *The Tempest* has this very beautiful musical shape, it's very concentrated and there's no long rambling narrative. It has been very difficult to find a structure in terms of dance and to find a way in which each character would move. Each day when I started with each specific character it took a while until I could find how, for example, Ariel, Caliban, Miranda or Ferdinand would move. But once that was established, the people in the Rambert company have so become those characters that whatever choreography I gave them came out in their own particular vocabulary of the character.

Recently I heard Neil Simon talking about writing for a film, and someone asked him if the incidents in the film had happened to him in real life. He answered 'Yes, they have all happened to me in real life, but not in the sequence in which I have used them, but what I have to do is to become my characters so completely that in any situation I would react as they would react'. This is what I have had to do with *The Tempest*: I have had to become each of the characters myself so that, in the musical structure relating to the choreographic structure, I could make each of these characters function as they do in the play.

Have you, for instance, taken the great soliloquies and turned them into solos?
They don't happen exactly where they happen in the play, but dance has this about it that it can eloquently say things, and a complex of images, that words cannot say. I haven't in fact had great difficulty with those great speeches of Prospero. What hasn't been easy are the subplots, which in the play itself I never find very interesting; those scenes with Antonio, Sebastian and the usurping brother who are there to give a focus to the strange wrath that Prospero has.

There are things that Shakespeare can do very quickly in words that are difficult to do in move-ment. For instance, in act 1 scene 2, when Miranda says 'How did we arrive on this island?', and in one speech he tells the entire preamble to the play, I have had to write things that I find visually exciting in that speech, also in Caliban's speech. I also wanted to show Ariel as a free spirit on the island before Prospero came there. I wanted to show Sycorax, who gave birth to Caliban, as a parallel to Prospero - she is a witch whereas he is a good white magician. I think I have put these

and all the other various inter-reacting themes almost as they happen in the play. I feel that it is very close to the spirit of the play without being a literal translation of it.

How did you work all this with your designer, Nadine Baylis?
Nadine, Arne and I have had a long association and we tend to communicate even in non-verbal ways, we tend to like the same things and feel the same way about things. So when all three of us were working with the Royal Danish Ballet, Nadine and I were sitting in an hotel right by the port in Copenhagen and it was the perfect atmosphere for *The Tempest*: the wild sea outside, the clouds scudding by, and all the noises in the masts of the ships. We both felt then that it was not going to be an historical recreation of the play but that it exists in all time and no time; it can be a very contemporary work.

It can also be a great piece of surrealism.
It's surreal and it's full of magic. I said in the beginning that I wanted magic, but the stripped-down magic of the oriental theatre which has always influenced me. By this I mean the theatre of Japan and China - Noh, Kabuki, Peking Opera and so on. I love the immaculate look of it, with its brilliant use of transformations and effects. So I said to Nadine, when I think of the goddesses, I would like those huge costumes of the Kabuki with yards and yards of China silk. In the play, for instance, Prospero says to Ariel 'Go dress yourself as a water nymph!', and I told Nadine that I wanted Ariel to be dressed like those courtesans in the Peking Opera with their long pillow sleeves, and that he should have the undulating walk in those high shoes. Then for the ladies of the court in Milan, that they should do one of those Chinese court dances. We discussed all of this use of oriental techniques. It has been said that the origin of *The Tempest* was one of those very ancient mystery plays which had the philosophy of Herakleitus in saying that one must give up everything so as to regain, and the Chinese philosophy of a sea voyage and returning, of loss and miraculous regaining of that which has been lost. Nadine has reflected this in her set which suggests wind, wave and which by a change of lighting, can become another part of the island, a grove, and all of these strange images, none of them real but which register on the inner mind.

This has been your first full-evening work. How do you feel about working on something of this length?

For me it's been a voyage of discovery, a new and entirely different way of working. Most of the works I have written previously have mainly been non-narrative, abstract, pure movement, although the majority of them had an emotional structure. In *The Tempest* I was not just relating to the music, I was using Shakespeare's structure, images and characters. I have found it totally consuming and an endless source of inspiration because each day, from the working situation with the dancers, something has been discovered. I have loved the luxury of having time to do things, because in this time one learns, as Shakespeare himself learned, that in such a long structure contrast is essential and that it is necessary to have a multi-level of interests going on at the same time. I hope that what Arne, Nadine and myself have done will work as a visual translation of *The Tempest* and that people, even if they don't know the play, will at least be absorbed in what's going on.

[Reprinted from *Dance and Dancers*, May 1979.]

The Tempest: Lucy Burge as Miranda, Thomas Yang as Caliban.   [TETLEY]

Rambert music

Noël Goodwin

It has been a feature of Ballet Rambert policy to encourage an often adventurous approach to music in its productions, notably in the early pioneering years of the 1930s, and especially since the major change in the company's character in 1966. Since that date alone, the list at the end of this book indicates almost 40 scores directly commissioned for works in repertory or workshop performance. They range in scope from the large-scale orchestral music of Arne Nordheim in two acts for Glen Tetley's *The Tempest* (1979) to others involving, perhaps, a small group or single instrumentalist for ten or twenty minutes. Such music comprises a vital element in the way most forms of dance in the theatre achieve their effect through the sense of sound as well as of sight.

From the beginning of this century, music began to acquire the status of an equal partner with the choreography in performance, and to serve an organic and not merely the decorative function it often did before. Igor Stravinsky (1882-1971), who did more than any other composer to bring this about, from the time of his discovery by Diaghilev, has best summed-up the desirable relationship between the two elements: 'Choreography must realise its own form, one independent of the musical form though measured to the musical unit. Its construction will be based on whatever correspondences the choreography may invent, but it must not seek merely to duplicate the line and beat of the music' (*Memories and Commentaries*, 1960).

Unless it is intentionally incidental to a choreographic conception, music usually marks out basic areas of time in which the dancing takes place. Beyond this, it can give additional depth and dimension to a ballet. It can add intensity of expression and firmness of shape to a plotless ballet, such as (to refer to recent Rambert repertory) the *Preludes and Song* by Christopher Bruce, or Richard Alston's *Landscape*. It can give emotional weight and a sense of direction to a dance-narrative like Tetley's *The Tempest* or Bruce's *Cruel Garden*. Sometimes it will prompt an instinctive, imaginative reflection of its own character and spirit, from the tragedy of Antony Tudor's *Dark Elegies* to the fantasy of Tetley's *Pierrot Lunaire* and Alston's *The Rite of Spring*.

The best of today's choreographers are not content simply to ride the surface of the music in their works, whether the music previously existed or was specially written. They will seek to understand and exploit the mutual relationship of eye and ear. They recognise that the appearance of any step in dancing can be changed by the stress of the musical rhythm – and not only by the rhythm alone, but also by whether the sound at a given point is loud or soft, the character of its instrumental timbre, the nature of its harmony and the quality of its expression. All these factors are capable of colouring the dancing the audience sees, as well as supporting it, and as they merge into a continuous momentum they help (or should help) to give coherence to the sequence of movement.

Attentive listening can correspondingly offer an insight into the dancing, as much as watching the dance should make one more keenly aware of the music. And, of course, just as the range of dance movement is no longer confined to the steps and style of 'classical' ballet, so the nature of music has itself expanded. Within the present repertory of Ballet Rambert alone, music will vary (perhaps in one programme, almost certainly within a week of performances) from simple tune-and-accompaniment at one extreme to intricate patterns of sound, possibly produced by electronic as well as other means. Stretching one's ears to accommodate this variety is part of the present experience of dance.

Ballet Rambert on occasion had recourse to gramophone records in its early years, but this was rare. However, no orchestra on regular engagement could be afforded until June 1945 at the King's Theatre, Hammersmith, a month after the war ended in Europe, helped by its first public subsidy from CEMA (Council for the Encouragement of Music and the Arts, precursor of the present Arts Council). Otherwise the music of the early Rambert years had to be written or arranged for one or two pianos, supplemented on special occasions by a necessary singer or instrumentalist, perhaps even a trio or quartet. A pick-up orchestra might be recruited for short but important West End or Manchester seasons, if funds allowed.

Several distinguished musicians nevertheless gave Ballet Rambert their practical support. Maude Lloyd, who writes elsewhere in this book, recalls Constant Lambert coming to play the second piano in an arrangement of the Walton music for Ashton's *Façade*, and the French violinist Jean Fournier as the solo violin with piano accompaniment in Chausson's *Poème* for Tudor's *Jardin aux Lilas* (1936). The Ashton ballet *Les Masques* (1933) involved a trio of oboe, bassoon and harp for the Poulenc music, and

Tudor's *Dark Elegies* (1937), rehearsed to a specific orchestral recording, was early performed to baritone and piano rather than the Mahlerian orchestra. Sometimes the simpler might be thought better, as with the Fauré piano pieces and songs for Andrée Howard's *La Fête Etrange* (1940), which were only later orchestrated for ballet performance.

What should now be remembered is that although the practical and economic problems of touring in the 1930s, before any system of public subsidy existed at all, forced Ballet Rambert (and other companies) into musical compromises, these were not allowed to inhibit their artistic enterprise. Choreographers turned to (and audiences were therefore introduced to, as a matter of course) such 'contemporary' composers of that time as Poulenc, Ravel and Honegger, or Bax, Benjamin and Berners among British names. There were also Bloch, Milhaud and Prokofiev, while audiences might encounter part of Holst's suite in Tudor's *The Planets* (1934) and would have been unaware that his *Dark Elegies* would acquire historical significance as the first-ever ballet to Mahler music.

After 1945, when an orchestra became possible on at least a semi-regular basis, Ballet Rambert was able to turn this to advantage in two directions. It could stage much more authentic versions of 19th century Romantic classics: the complete *Giselle* in 1946, *Coppélia* in 1957 and *La Sylphide* in 1960, and supplement these with a memorable *Don Quixote* in 1962. It could also give a richer musical resource to new works such as Andrée Howard's *The Sailor's Return* (1947), for which Arthur Oldham's music was the the first-ever full-length score for ballet by a British composer (anticipating by ten years Benjamin Britten's *The Prince of the Pagodas* for John Cranko), and to the first exciting works by the emerging Norman Morrice, with music by Surinach, Shostakovich and others.

Among the composers to whom Morrice turned at this time was the London-born Leonard Salzedo (b 1921), who not only wrote the music for two early Morrice ballets, *The Travellers* (1963) and *Realms of Choice* (1965) (and followed these with *Hazard* in 1967 and *The Empty Suit* in 1970), but became the first Music Director for the company after it was re-formed on a modern dance basis in 1966. Salzedo stayed in that capacity for six years, playing an important part in establishing the new identity for Ballet Rambert. He has been succeeded in turn by Colin Metters in 1972, Adam Gatehouse in 1974, Charles Darden in 1978 and Nicholas Carr in 1980.

A condition of the Musicians' Union agreement

Leonard Salzedo.

Adam Gatehouse.

94

to the company's change of character in 1966 was the continued employment of musicians as an ensemble for live performance. The repertory, however, was no longer based on the conventional pit orchestra, and it became necessary to form and develop a much more flexible ensemble, with skilled players responsive to the demands of modern composers. I recall Salzedo mentioning to me, not long after his appointment as Music Director, that his musical responsibility ranged from Vivaldi to Schoenberg and Stockhausen. He believed that this development, as well as the possibility of inviting more composers to write original works for dance had vitally helped to change attitudes to dance among musicians generally.

During the 1970s the players who performed with Ballet Rambert found increasing challenges to their artistry and technique in the repertory that confronted them. They acquired an identity of their own as the Mercury Ensemble, and from time to time they gave separate concerts and occasional broadcasts, although the schedule of a busy touring company normally allows little opportunity for such extra activities. What did happen was the Mercury Ensemble became more constant in its personnel, many players returning from season to season. They were encouraged to become more integrated with the dancers, and more involved during rehearsal with the presentation and performance on stage, from which the pit position usually hides them.

Adam Gatehouse, in an interview after his four years as Music Director, made a comment to me which I do not think has been better put: 'I passionately believe that you can have uncompromisingly high quality of music in dance, and this starts with a good class pianist. I was very lucky in this respect to have Carlos Miranda, one of the best pianists for class I've heard anywhere. It affects the whole musicality of approach among the dancers, which is carried over to the repertory. There's so much in the routine of a dancer's life which can beat

Charles Darden rehearsing The Mercury Ensemble.

down on musicality, and a bad class pianist, day in and day out for months and years, will just close a dancer's ears. Working with tape has other problems because, by the very nature of it, every repeat performance is exactly the same as the one before, and you just stop listening after a while. This is why live music for dance can transform the whole nature of it and its impact' (*Dance and Dancers*, Oct. 1978).

Especially where pre-existing music is used for choreographic purposes it cannot be too strongly emphasised, in my view, that the level of choreographic imagination must never be lower than that of the music. It can be better than its music, but it cannot afford to be lesser, or the dancing will be submerged. Which is why optimum results should occur when original music and original choreography are created in collaboration. What use the choreographer makes of music is his own decision. In theory, at least, all music can be danceable to some extent, but in the most potent or rewarding combinations of music and dance, the two elements together make something *more* than, and *different* from, their separate qualities. They are parallel conceptions, and it is the mutual enrichment of one by the other which brings, from the art of dance in the theatre, the most exciting rewards for performers and audiences alike.

Nicholas Carr.

The Rite of Spring: Sally Owen as the Chosen One. [ALSTON]

A decade of digs

Sally Owen

In the days before I discovered thermal underwear there was Aberdeen. I remember arriving in gentle snow during an oil tanker strike. Unaware of how horrible things would be that week some of us played snowballs on a little green in front of the theatre. In the theatre there was no hot water, no heating until half an hour before the show, and nobody washed for a week. In class everyone was wearing woolly hats and gloves and so many pairs of tights that you couldn't bend your knees. Julia Blaikie's protest was to keep a fur coat on during the performance of *tutti frutti*. Still the snow came down. The street leading to the digs was lined with cars buried in snow and in the digs themselves there was ice on the bedroom window. Jennie Staples and I were sharing a room and there was a tiny blow-heater and we used to take it in turns to stand in front of it and let the heat circulate up our nighties and then jump quickly into bed. Breakfasts there were good and enormous, served by the landlady who wore a short-sleeved cotton dress and a pinny and who made a habit of turning off the one-bar electric heater saying 'Och, you've had enough heat now'. There was one night when we

attempted to take a bath but by the time it was full the water was cold.

Then there was the visit to the temporary tent inside the Manchester Stock Exchange before the new theatre was built. Solid marble surrounds and no heating. While the dancers suffered on stage in all-over body tights the audience were issued with blankets. Our stage manager solved his circulation problem by buying a pair of roller skates and skating round the tent in never-ending circles.

Poland was a good tour. My first foreign tour. Apart from the fact that I cannot remember eating at all or ever seeing food in shops, it was nice because we travelled on a coach from city to city so we could see the countryside. Usually on a foreign tour you just fly into a city, perform and then fly out again. You might see a bit of the city itself but nothing more. I was very impressed by the hotel rooms at Lodz. Lucy Burge and I had this huge suite - one enormous room with candelabra and enormous palms, a marble bathroom and a separate bedroom - such luxury, incredible.

My general impressions of touring: a feeling like that of a child, far from the responsibilities and demands of home, an unreal situation which at times makes any kind of personal or social relationship very difficult.

The closeness of the company group therefore becomes very important and this intimacy has increased with the use of self-catering flats or cottages. There are so few '5 star theatrical digs' left now and Bed and Breakfast places don't usually cater for the hours dancers keep (breakfast tends to finish at 8.30 am). Staying together, talking together (which we normally have little time for) in a place which is 'ours', if only for a week, makes our lives, I think, a little more normal. Many dancers, including myself, look on touring with the dread of being uprooted once again, but even though in time it is wearing, I would not have missed the experience for the world.

Dancers' attitudes have changed; nowadays no one would accept the conditions in Aberdeen and Manchester. But nonetheless dancers are slow to change their lot.

'In the days before I discovered thermal underwear there was Aberdeen . . .'
Sally Owen.

Then and now

William Ferguson

Thirty-three years is a long time to work for one company in the theatrical profession.

I joined Ballet Rambert in 1948 after the company had returned from an eighteen month tour of Australia and New Zealand. I was engaged to prepare the scenery and props in order to commence touring again in England – a formidable task when I saw the pitiful state they were in. There was nowhere to work other than some waste ground in Notting Hill Gate, just across from the Mercury Theatre. Wood and canvas and other materials were in short supply, not to mention money as there were no Arts Council grants in those days.

My first date was at the Theatre Royal, Bath, for the Festival, after which the company returned to the Mercury Theatre for a short season; this meant adapting the scenery to fit the very small stage of the theatre. Life became hectic with Madame Rambert driving and encouraging her dancers and myself into action. Those early days were very hard for everyone. Time was short, money was short – even tempers.

Then began the many years of touring in Great Britain and abroad. Five to six tons of scenery had

William Ferguson.

to be loaded onto lorries, then unloaded and reloaded into railway trucks. On arrival at each town the trucks had to be unloaded and reloaded into lorries and taken to the theatre and then transferred to the stage working area. This would go on for about forty-eight weeks of the year and one felt completely exhausted at the end of a tour. We would then return to London and the company would start rehearsals for new ballets, and with fine weather and no complaints from the neighbours I was able to build sets out in the roadway (Ladbroke Road being a very quiet thoroughfare in those days), having no room in the small stores.

As time went by the company expanded and Madame introduced some of the classical ballets into the repertoire: *Coppélia*, *La Sylphide* and *Don Quixote*. The company had now attained a high artistic standard of dancing and production and to maintain these standards required a great deal of hard work and dedication from everyone.

One of the most important contributions to the staging of ballet is lighting. One has to be able to create an atmosphere to enhance the ballet. This entailed a wide spectrum of colour and lantern variations and all this had to be done in those early days with what equipment was available at each theatre. Some had a fair amount, others had very little. As years went by I managed to purchase certain types of lanterns to augment the theatres' own lighting which was an enormous advantage in small theatres where this was very limited.

In 1966 the company's policy changed completely: dancing the classics was discontinued and the concentration was on modern dance by new choreographers, designers and composers. New techniques were devised in the construction of scenery – metal and plastic replacing wood and canvas; a completely new approach to lighting and sound came into use. All this required extra equipment and stage technicians to operate and maintain it. Road transport was being extensively used for moving scenery about the country. This resulted in less handling, time, wear and tear.

What of the present? Now the company has its own headquarters in Chiswick consisting of rehearsal rooms, workshops, offices and wardrobe, instead of having to work in cold church halls or scout huts, and I no longer have to worry about the neighbours' complaints. Yes, conditions have improved over the years, and I am pleased to have played a small part in the company's history, but none of my help would have been possible without the full co-operation of everyone concerned, plus a very understanding wife.

Ballet Rambert Repertory

YEAR	TITLE	CHOREOGRAPHER	COMPOSER	DESIGNER
1926	*A Tragedy of Fashion*	Ashton	E. Goossens	Fedorovitch
1927	*Faery Queen* (Dances in)	Ashton	Purcell	
1928	*Les Petits Riens*	Ashton	Mozart	
	Leda and the Swan	Ashton	Gluck	Chappell
1929	*Mars and Venus*	Ashton	Scarlatti	Norris
	The Tale of a Lamb	Salaman	Grovlez	Salaman
1930	*Capriol Suite*	Ashton	Warlock	Chappell
	Our Lady's Juggler	Salaman	Respighi	Salaman
	Les Sylphides (with Karsavina)	Fokine	Chopin	
	Le Rugby	Salaman	Poulenc	Salaman
	Le Spectre de la Rose (with Karsavina)	Fokine	Weber	Bakst (costumes)
	Le Carnaval (with Karsavina and Woizikovski)	Fokine	Schumann	Bakst (costumes)
	Le Cricket	Salaman	Benjamin	Salaman
	A Florentine Picture	Ashton	Corelli	after Botticelli
1931	*Le Boxing*	Salaman	Berners	Chappell
	La Péri (with Markova)	Ashton	Dukas	Chappell
	Aurora's Wedding (with Markova)	Petipa	Tchaikovsky	
	L'Après-midi d'un Faune	Nijinsky	Debussy	Bakst
	Façade (Camargo production with Markova)	Ashton	Walton	Armstrong
	Swan Lake (with Markova)	Petipa/Ivanov	Tchaikovsky	
	Waterloo and Crimea (with Karsavina and Woizikovski)	Salaman	Berners	Salaman
	Mercury (with Karsavina)	Ashton	Satie	Chappell
	The Lady of Shalott	Ashton	Sibelius	Chappell
	Cross-Garter'd	Tudor	Frescobaldi	after Burnacini
	The Tartans	Ashton	Chappell	Boyce
1932	*Mr. Roll's Quadrilles*	Tudor	Old Music	Salaman
	Lysistrata	Tudor	Prokofiev	Chappell
	The Garden	Salaman	Murrill	Salaman
	Unbowed	Patrick	Bax	Stevenson
	Foyer de Danse (with Markova)	Ashton	Berners	Chappell after Degas
1933	*Pavane pour une Infante Défunte*	Ashton	Ravel	Stevenson
	Les Masques (with Markova)	Ashton	Poulenc	Fedorovitch
	Atalanta of the East	Ashton	Eastern (mus. arr)	Chappell
	Pavane pour une Infante Défunte	Tudor	Ravel	Stevenson
	Our Lady's Juggler	Howard/Salaman	Respighi	Salaman/Howard
	Récamier	Ashton	Schubert	Chappell
1934	*Mermaid*	Howard/Salaman	Ravel	Howard
	Paramour (Done with costumes by John Lear in O.U.D.S. Production of 'Dr. Faustus')	Tudor	Boyce	Chappell
	Bar aux Folies-Bergère (with Markova)	De Valois	Chabrier	Chappell after Manet
	Mephisto Valse (with Markova)	Ashton	Liszt	Fedorovitch
	Alcina Suite	Howard	Handel	Howard
	The Planets (with Kyra Nijinsky)	Tudor	Holst	Stevenson
1935	*Cinderella*	Howard	Weber	Howard
	Valentine's Eve	Ashton	Ravel	Fedorovitch
	The Descent of Hebe	Tudor	Bloch	Benois
	Circus Wings	Salaman	Milhaud	Salaman
	The Rape of the Lock	Howard	Haydn	Howard
1936	*Jardin aux Lilas*	Tudor	Chausson	Stevenson
	Passionate Pavane (New version)	Ashton	Dowland	Chappell
	La Muse s'Amuse	Howard	De Sévérac	Howard

1937	*Dark Elegies*	Tudor	Mahler	Nadia Benois
	Death and the Maiden	Howard	Schubert	Howard
	Suite of Airs	Tudor	Purcell	Nadia Benois
	Pavane pour une Infante Défunte	Bentley Stone	Ravel	Stevenson
	Cross-Garter'd	Toye	Frescobaldi	after Burnacini
1938	*The Tartans*	Staff	Boyce	Chappell
	Croquis de Mercure	Howard	Satie	Howard
	La Péri	Staff	Dukas	Nadia Benois
	Judgment of Paris (London Ballet Production)	Tudor	Weill	Laing
	Soirée Musicale (London Ballet Production)	Tudor	Rossini/Britten	Stevenson
	Valse Finale	Gore	Ravel	Fedorovitch
	Gala Performance (London Ballet Production)	Tudor	Prokofiev	Stevenson
	Paris-Soir	Gore	Poulenc	Swinstead-Smith
1939	*Lady into Fox*	Howard	Honegger	Nadia Benois
	Czernyana	Staff	Czerny	Swinstead-Smith
	Peter and the Wolf	Staff	Prokofiev	Sheppard
1940	*Le Pas des Déesses* (London Ballet Production)	Lester	Pugni	Guthrie/Stevenson
	Cap Over Mill	Gore	Bate	Nadia Benois
	Love in Idleness (London Ballet Production)	Bidmead	Purcell	Guthrie
	La Fête Etrange (London Ballet Production)	Howard	Fauré	Fedorovitch
	Enigma Variations	Staff	Elgar	Sheppard
	Bartlemas Dances (Oxford University Ballet Club Production)	Gore	Holst	Chappell
	Czerny 2	Staff	Czerny	Swinstead-Smith
	Pavane pour une Infante Défunte	Staff	Ravel	Stevenson
	Confessional (O.U. Ballet Club Production)	Gore	Sibelius	Howard
1943	*Carnival of Animals*	Howard	Saint-Saëns	Howard
	Flamenco	Brunelleschi	Gerhard	Stevenson
	The Fugitive	Howard	Salzedo	Stevenson
1944	*Simple Symphony*	Gore	Britten	Wilson
1945	*Giselle Act II*	Coralli/Perrot	Adam	Stevenson
	Un Songe	Staff	Lekeu	Wilson
1946	*Mr. Punch*	Gore	Oldham	Wilson
	Giselle (Complete)	Coralli/Perrot	Adam	Stevenson
1947	*The Sailor's Return*	Howard	Oldham	Howard
	Plaisance	Gore	Rossini	Cordwell
	Concerto Burlesco	Gore	Bartok	Swinstead-Smith
1948	*Nutcracker Suite*	Ivanov	Tchaikovsky	Cordwell
	Winter Night	Gore	Rachmaninov	Rowell
1949	*Fireflies*	Gore	Brahms/Paganini	Wilson
	Antonia	Gore	Sibelius	Cordwell
1950	*The Eve of St. Agnes*	Paltenghi	Franck	Furse
	Prismatic Variations	Paltenghi	Beethoven	Kernot
1951	*House of Cards*	Paltenghi	Monteverdi	Hurry
	Fate's Revenge	Paltenghi	Tranchell	Ferns
	Canterbury Prologue	Paltenghi	Racine Fricker	Burra
1952	*Movimientos* (Ballet Workshop Production)	Charnley	Hobson	Smith/Lingwood
	Past Recalled (Ballet Workshop Production)	Carter	Bloch	McDowell
	Carnival of Animals (New version)	Bates	Saint-Saëns	Biggar/Montlake
1954	*Love Knots*	Carter	Hummel	Ferns
	Life and Death of Lola Montez (Ballet Workshop Production)	Carter	Verdi	McDowell
	Variations on a Theme	Cranko	Britten	Rowell
1955	*Laiderette*	MacMillan	Martin	Rowell
	Pas des Déesses	Joffrey	Field	Delaney
	Persephone	Joffrey	Vivaldi	Wich
1956	*Coppélia* (*Act III*)	Ivanov	Delibes	Doboujinsky
	The Mirror	Yerrell	Larsen	Jones
1957	*Coppélia* (Complete)	Ivanov	Delibes	Doboujinsky
	Conte Fantastique	Howard	Caplet	Pride
1958	*Epithalame*	Mendel	Guillaume	Mendel
	Two Brothers	Morrice	Dohnanyi	Koltai
1959	*Hazana*	Morrice	Surinach	Koltai
	La Reja	Cranko	Scarlatti	Toms

Year	Title	Choreographer	Composer	Designer
1960	The Wise Monkeys	Morrice	Shostakovitch	Adron
	La Sylphide	Bournonville	Lovenskjold	C. & R. Ironside
1961	Night Shadow	Balanchine	Rieti/Bellini	Stone
	A Place in the Desert	Morrice	Surinach	Koltai
1962	Don Quixote	Gorsky/Zakharoff	Minkus	Voytek
	Conflicts	Morrice	Bloch	Koltai
1963	Les Sylphides	Fokine	Chopin	Stone
	The Travellers	Morrice	Salzedo	Koltai
1964	Sweet Dancer	Gore	Martin	Cordwell
	Cul-de-Sac	Morrice	Whelen	Koltai
1965	Giselle (New Production)	Coralli/Perrot	Adam	Farmer
	Realms of Choice	Morrice	Salzedo	Baylis
1966	Diversities	Taylor	Badings	Koltai
	Singular Moves	Knott	Lasry/Bachet	Kirkpatrick
	Company re-formed (18/7/1966)			
	Numéros	Lacotte		
	Time Base	Chesworth	Lutoslawski	Baylis
	Intermède	Lacotte	Vivaldi	Corre
	Night Island	Van Dantzig	Debussy	Van Schayk
1967	Pierrot Lunaire	Tetley	Schoenberg	Ter-Arutunian
	Ricercare	Tetley	Seter	Ter-Arutunian
	Collaboration I	Ballet Rambert/Central School of Art & Design		
	Inochi	Toguri		Napier
	Mechos	Knott	Philipot/Schaeffer	Jordan
	Tic-Tack	Chesworth	Kreisler/Rachmaninoff	Chesworth
	Death by Dimensions	North	Parsons	Lipp
	The Judas Figures	Early	Nono	Garrard
	Inochi	Toguri		Napier
	Deserts	Sokolow	Varèse	Sokolow
	Hazard	Morrice	Salzedo	Baylis
	L'Après-midi d'un Faune (revival)	Nijinsky	Debussy	Baylis
	Freefall	Tetley	Schubel	Tetley
	Ziggurat	Tetley	Stockhausen	Baylis
1968	'H'	Chesworth	Penderecki	Chesworth
	Collaboration II	Ballet Rambert/Central School of Art & Design		
	Remembered Motion	Moore	Fox	Moore
	Throughway	Popescu	Vorhaus	Jarman
	Curiouser and Curiouser	Knott	Carter	Parsons
	Solo	Roope	Goehr	
	The Little Dog Laughed	Taylor	Brown	Burton
	Tic-Tack	Chesworth	Kreisler/Rachmaninoff	Chesworth
	Remembered Motion	Moore	Fox	Moore
	Them & Us	Morrice	Xenakis	Baylis
	1-2-3	Morrice	Orgad	Morrice
	The Act	Hodes	Page-Johnson	Hodes
	Pawn to King 5	Chesworth	Pink Floyd	Carney/Chesworth
	Embrace Tiger and Return to Mountain	Tetley	Subotnick	Baylis
1969	Pastorale Variée	Morrice	Ben Haim	Baylis
	George Frideric	Bruce	Handel	Napier
	Blind-Sight	Morrice	Downes	Baylis
	Living Space	Bruce	Cockburn	Baylis
1970	Bertram Batell's Sideshow	Various	Various	Cazalet
	Opus '65	Sokolow	Macero	Sokolow
	Four According	Chesworth	Bacewicz	Cazalet
	The Empty Suit	Morrice	Salzedo	Morrice
	'Tis Goodly Sport	Taylor	16th Century Music	Cazalet
1971	Metaflow	Scoglio	Rudnik/Malovec	Cazalet
	Wings	Bruce	Downes	Bruce
	That is the Show	Morrice	Berio	Baylis
	Solo	Morrice	Downes	Baylis
	Rag Dances	Tetley	Hymas	Baylis

Year	Title			
1972	Dance for New Dimensions			
	'for these who die as cattle'	Bruce		Baylis
	This seems to be my Life	Curtis	Salzedo	
	Ad Hoc	Chesworth	Improvised	
	Ladies Ladies	Morrice	Hymas	Baylis
	4 Pieces for 6 Dancers	Law	Various	Baylis
	Theme and Variations	Jones	Modern Jazz Quartet	Baylis
	Full Circle	Avrahami	Bartok	Baylis
	Stop-Over	Scoglio	Takemitsu	Baylis
	Sonata for Two	Taylor	Prokofiev	Baylis
	Pattern for an Escalator	Chesworth	Harvey	Baylis
	Considering the Lilies	Lubovitch	Bach	Lubovitch
	Listen to the Music	Taylor	Hymas	Beavan
	Totems	Jones	Gibbs	Don
1973	There was a Time (Fanfare for Europe)	Bruce	Hodgson	Baylis
	Dance for New Dimensions			
	Magic Theatre – not for everyone	Warren	Le Fanu	Ringwood
	Interim 1, 2 and 3	Hassall	Lockwood/Joplin	Ringwood
	Les Saltimbanques	Scoglio	Cowie	
	Cantate	Jones	Gibbs	Ringwood
	yesterday and yesterday	Blaikie	Sound montage	Blaikie/Fey
	Funky	Avrahami	Emerson, Lake and Palmer	Morris
	Ballet (untitled)	Carroll	Pehkonen	Bjornsson/Blane
	The whole is made up of single units	Prestidge	Metcalfe	Murray-Clark
	tutti-frutti	Falco	Alcantara	Katz
	Isolde	Morrice	Lewis	Baylis
	Duets	Bruce	Hodgson	Baylis
1974	Weekend	Bruce	Hodgson	Bruce
	Spindrift	Morrice	Lewis	Kelly
	Escaras	Alum	Krauze/Szalonek	Alum
	Almost an Echo	Taylor	Milhaud	Bryant
	Project 6354/9116 Mk II	Chesworth	Vuorenjuuri	Baylis
1975	The Parades Gone by	Kemp	Various	Kornilof
	Running Figures	North	Burgon	Farmer
	Baby	Marcuse	Lambert	Murray-Clark
	The Night Dances	Scoglio	Downes	Gill
	Table	Keuter	Ravel	Nobbe
	Musete di Taverni	Keuter	Couperin	Keuter
	Freefall (Revival)	Tetley	Schubel	Baylis (new desig
	Ancient Voices of Children	Bruce	Crumb	Baylis
	Take A Running Jump	Various	Various	Murray-Clark
1976	Collaboration III	Ballet Rambert/Central School of Art & Design		
	Steppes	Brown	Scott	Gilkes
	Hot Air	Warren	Winter	Durrant
	There is a dream that is dreaming me	Blaikie	Miranda	Turner/Harris
	Two minutes and fifty seconds . . .	Owen	New Orleans Wanderers	Fey
	Fixations	Imre	Sound collage	Harris/Turner
	The Small Hours	Scoglio	Scarlatti	Scoglio
	Performance	Smith	Various	
	5–4–3–2–1	Westerdijk	Hooper	Harris
	Widdershins	Carroll	Eaton	Coskinas/Gilkes
	Four Working Songs	Marcuse	Miranda	Coskinas
	Moveable Garden	Tetley	Foss	Baylis
	Black Angels	Bruce	Crumb	Baylis
	Cradle (retitled The Sea Whisper'd Me)	Morrice	Miranda	Macfarlane
	Reflections	North	Blake	Baylis
	Girl with Straw Hat	Bruce	Brahms	Baylis
	Window	Sugihara	Kottke/Fahy/Lang	Durrant
	Promenade	Bruce	Bach	Baylis
	Musical Offering	Imre	Bach, arr. Lambert	Imre/Fey

Year	Title			
1977	Collaboration IV	Ballet Rambert/Central School of Art & Design		
	Kuyaiki	Sherwood	Pre Columbian Folk Music	Gregory
	The Accident	Imre	Sound collage	Ashard
	The Pool	Warren	Lewis	Durrant
	Nowhere to Go	Loretz	Weston	West
	Images for Two	Frankel	Balinese Gamelan Music	Gregory
	Side by Side	Fernandez	Schoenberg	Ashard
	Episode One	Flier	Posselt	Baylis
	Echoes of a Night Sky	Bruce	Crumb	Baylis
	Frames, Pulse and Interruptions	Flier	Birtwistle	Baylis
	Smiling Immortal	Morrice	Harvey	Macfarlane
	Cruel Garden	Bruce/Kemp	Miranda	Koltai/Kemp
	Sleeping Birds	Sugihara	Brahms	Durrant (redes. Baylis)
1978	Praeludium	Tetley	Webern	Baylis
	Laocoon	Imre	Sound collage	Baylis
	Nuthouse Stomp	Warren	Waller/Miller	Ringwood
	Workshop Season	Riverside Studios		
	Le Petit Prince	Loretz	Jazz collage	Fey
	Fourfold	Vardi	Shostakovich	Baylis
	Forgotten Songs	Sherwood	Debussy	Sherwood
	Longing	Vardi	Ginastera	Kvartz
	Dancers – a film	Dir: Chesworth/Hart/Yamazaki		
1979	Echoi	Flier	Foss/Vivaldi	Baylis
	The Tempest	Tetley	Nordheim	Baylis
	Workshop Season	Riverside Studios		
	Naiades	Ward	Alwyn	Fey
	Still Life	Hart	Mozart	
	Li-los	Loretz	Dance band music	Fey
	I'll Be In Touch	Owen/Warren	Parker/Betjeman	Stedham
	The Dinner	Vardi	Carr	Fey
	Cakes and ale . . . and ale	Vardi/Burge/Owen/ Yang/Warren	Brass collage	Freedman
	The Shadow of Ideas	Paoluzi	Vivaldi/Pert/Curran	Tappenden
	Jesus' Blood Never Failed Me Yet	Fernandez	Bryars	Penalva
	Duet for Four	Dickie	Feldman	Fey
	Moments for Nothing	Wraith	Hinnigan	
	Changes	Bergese	Muldowney	da Costa
	Celebration	Davies	arr. Carr	Fey
	Night With Waning Moon	Bruce	Crumb	Marre
	Sidewalk	Bruce	Lambert	Marre
1980	Bell High	Alston	Maxwell Davies	Mumford
	Workshop Season	Riverside Studios		
	Passing Through	Bethune	Poulenc	Bethune, ass. by Jobst
	Changing Spot	Loretz	Bach	Freeman
	Surface Values	Clark	Clare	
	summer haze	Ho	Chopin	Fey
	". . . then we shall truly dance"	Ward	Gibran	Fey
	Octuor	Vardi	Stravinsky	Fey
	Preludes and Song	Bruce	Hymas	Marre
	Landscape	Alston	Vaughan Williams	Mumford
	Rainbow Ripples	Alston	Amirkhanian/Green	Buckland
1981	Figures of Wind	Keuter	Albinoni/Torelli/ Manfredini	Keuter/Scarlett
	Room to Dance	Keuter	Villa-Lobos	Bowen/Scarlett
	The Rite of Spring	Alston	Stravinsky	Mumford/Guyon
	Paper Sunday	Owen	Bach	Owen
	Dancing Day	Bruce	Holst	Bruce
	Workshop Season	Riverside Studios		
	One or the Other	Becque	Taylor	
	Untitled Duet	Clark		
	Four Solos to Guitar Music	Ward	Villa-Lobos/Henze	Fey
	Unsuitable Case	Owen	Hinnigan/Strauss	Fey
	Solus	Ham	Rogers	
	Twice Three	Bethune	Carr	Bethune
	Soliloquy	Fernandez	Debussy	Ashard
	Music Case	Owen		
	All The Lonely People	Price	Swithinbank	
	Ghost Dances	Bruce	South American Folk Songs	Bruce/Scarlett
	Lonely Town, Lonely Street	North	Withers	Storer

List of artists and staff

(b) Ballet Master/Ballet Mistress
(ch) Choreographer
(comp) Composer
(chor) Choreologist
(d) Dancer
(des) Designer
(dir) Director
(ld) Lighting Designer
(m) Administrators/Publicity/Secretaries
(mus) Conductors/Pianists
(sm) Stage Management
(w) Wardrobe

A

Addams, C. (d)
Adron, R. (des)
Alcantara, B. (comp)
Aldous, L. (d)
Allen, J. (d)
Allen, S. (sm)
Alletson, S. (d)
Alston, R. (ch)
Alum, M. (ch)
Anderson, V. (d)
Anderton, J. (ld-sm)
Andrewes, J. (d)
Andrewes, P. (m)
Argyle, P. (d)
Armstrong, J. (des)
Arnold, J. (d)
Arova, S. (d)
Ash, N. (d)
Ashley, A. (d)
Ashton, F. (d-ch)
Ashworth, P. (d)
Asscherick, A. (d)
Attenborough, J. (m)
Avrahami, G. (d)

B

Balanchine, G. (ch)
Baldwin, M. (d)
Banks, J. (d)
Bannerman, K. (d)
Banting, J. (des)
Barbour, D. (sm)
Barrett, C. (d)
Barton, L. (d)
Bates, C. (d-ch)
Baylis, N. (des)
Bayston, M. (d)
Beasley, C. (d)
Beaumont, P. (b)
Beavan, J. (des)
Becque, C. (d)
Belair, A. (d)
Bell, B. (d)
Ben-Ari, N. (d)
Benbow, E. (mus)
Bennett, A. (d)
Benois, N. (des)

Benoit, J. (d)
Bergese, M. (ch)
Bethune, L. (d)
Bidmead, C. (d-ch)
Biggar, H. (des-w)
Birtwistle, H. (comp)
Black, K. (m)
Black, M. (d)
Blaikie, J. (d)
Boam, M. (d)
Bocquet, P. (des)
Boshoff, P. (d)
Bougaard, C. (d)
Bourne, V. (m)
Bowen, E. (m)
Bowen, R. (des)
Bowers, J. (d)
Boyd, C. (d)
Bradford, H. (mus)
Bradshaw, P. (sm)
Brae, J. (d)
Bragg, N. (sm)
Bryant, J. (des)
Briar, S. (d)
Briggs, V. (d)
Brill, M. (ld-sm)
Bromwich, F. (m)
Brookes, A. (d)
Brown, B. (d)
Brown, R. (mus)
Bruce, C. (d-ch-assoc dir)
Brunelleschi, E. (ch)
Brusa, A. (d)
Buckland, D. (des)
Burge, L. (d)
Burge, N. (sm)
Burgon, G. (comp)
Burra, E. (des)
Buttery, D. (d)
Byrne, S. (d)
Byron, J. (d)

C

Callaghan, D. (d)
Carl, J. (des)
Carney, M. (des)
Carr, L. (m)

Carr, N. (mus)
Carroll, N. (d)
Carter, J. (ch)
Carty, F. (d)
Cassie, P. (d)
Caswell, R. (ld-sm)
Cazalet, P. (d-des)
Cerda, E. (d)
Chappell, A. (d)
Chappell, W. (d-des)
Chard, K. (d)
Charnley, M. (ch)
Chase, A. (d)
Chesworth, J. (d-ch-dir)
Christie, E. (d)
Clark, C. (m)
Clark, M. (d)
Clayden, P. (d)
Clogstoun, P. (d)
Cockburn, R. (comp)
Collis, M. (d)
Cooper, S. (d)
Cooper, W. (w)
Corbett, G. (mus)
Cordwell, H. (d-des)
Cornford, H. (d)
Corre, J. J. (des)
Coster, G. (d)
Courtney, C. (d)
Cowie, E. (comp)
Craig, H. (d)
Craig, S. (d)
Cranko, J. (ch)
Crookes, J. (d)
Crosby, R. (sm)
Cuff, B. (d)
Cunliffe, A. (d)
Cunliffe, E. (chor)
Cunningham, F. (d)
Curtis, P. (d)

D

Da Costa, L. (des)
Dalrymple, J. (d)
Darden, C. (mus)
Davey, J. (d)

Davidson, G. (b)
Davidson, M. (sm)
Davies, S. (w)
Davies, S. (ch)
D'Avray, T. (d)
De Graef, M. (d)
Delaney, E. (des)
De Ligniere, A. (b-d)
De Marigny, M. (d)
De Mille, A. (d)
Dering, D. (d)
Detot, G. (d)
De Valois, N. (ch)
Dickie, A. (d)
Dixon, N. (d)
Dixon, S. (d)
Doboujinsky, M. (des)
Dodd, J. (d)
Dodds, V. (d)
Don, R. (des)
Doone, R. (d)
Dowey, J. (m)
Downes, B. (comp)
Draisey, D. (d)
Draper, C. (sm)
Draper, L. (d)
Dukes, L. (d)
Dumas, R. (d)
Durrant, H. (des)
Dyer, P. (d)
Dyson, C. (d)

E

Edsall, J. (w)
Edwards, L. (d)
Einrem, S. (d)
Ellen, S. (ld-sm)
Ellenberg, D. (mus)
Ellis, D. (d-assoc dir)
Elvin, V. (d)
Evans, P. (m)

F

Falco, L. (ch)
Farmer, P. (des)
Fedorovitch, S. (des)

Ferguson, W. (*sm*)
Fernandez, N. (*d*)
Ferns, R. (*des*)
Fey, C. (*d-w*)
Field, J. (*d*)
Field, M. (*d*)
Flier, J. (*ch*)
Flindt, F. (*d*)
Fonteyn, M. (*d*)
Forbes, H. (*d*)
Foster, P. (*d*)
Fox, M. (*comp*)
Franca, C. (*d*)
Frankel, D. (*choreologist*)
Franklin-White, P. (*d*)
Fraser, P. (*d*)
Furse, L. (*des*)

G

Gable, C. (*d*)
Gaden, P. (*d*)
Gamble, R. (*d*)
Garbutt, S. (*b-chor*)
Garman, J. (*d*)
Gatehouse, A. (*mus*)
Gee, A. (*d*)
Gerhard, R. (*comp*)
Gibbs, L. (*d*)
Gibbs, M. (*comp*)
Gibson, N. (*d*)
Gilbert, T. (*d*)
Gill, L. (*des*)
Gilmour, G. (*d*)
Gilmour, S. (*d*)
Gilpin, J. (*d*)
Glanville, M. (*sm*)
'Goldie'. (*mus*)
Goldwyn, B. (*d*)
Golovina, N. (*d*)
Gore, W. (*d-ch*)
Gornell, M. (*d*)
Gould, D. (*d*)
Gow, D. (*d*)
Graeme, J. (*d-b*)
Grant, H. (*d*)
Greene, J. (*m*)
Greet, J. (*d*)
Griffin, P. (*sm*)
Grimes, B. (*d*)
Gritti, E. (*d*)
Gush, P. (*w*)
Guthrie, J. (*des*)
Guyon, A. (*des*)

H

Halcrow, R. (*mus*)
Ham, R. (*d*)
Hamilton, G. (*d*)
Hamilton, L. (*sm*)
Hamlyn, B. (*d*)
Hammond, W. (*sm*)
Harbour, A. (*d*)
Harcot, P. (*d*)

Hardie, A. (*w*)
Hardwick, J. (*d*)
Hare, J. (*d*)
Harrold, R. (*d*)
Hart, D. (*d*)
Hart, P. (*sm*)
Harvey, J. (*comp*)
Harvey, N. (*d*)
Hassall, N. (*d-ch*)
Haughton, C. (*d*)
Hawkins, M. (*d*)
Hayden, S. (*d*)
Helpmann, R. (*d*)
Heritage, S. (*d*)
Hersey, D. (*ld*)
Hill, M. (*d*)
Hindmarch, C. (*d*)
Hinton, P. (*d*)
Ho, M. (*d*)
Hobson, M. (*comp*)
Hodes, L. (*ch*)
Hodgson, B. (*comp*)
Hodiak, K. (*d*)
Hogan, M. (*d*)
Holland, R. (*d*)
Hollings, E. (*d*)
Holmes, M. (*d*)
Honore, J. (*d*)
Hopkins, N. (*d*)
Horn, A. (*d*)
Hought, O. (*d*)
Howard, A. (*d-ch-des*)
Hughes, L. (*d*)
Hughes, M. (*m*)
Hunt, D. (*d*)
Hurry, L. (*des*)
Hyman, P. (*d*)
Hymas, A. (*mus-comp*)
Hynd, R. (*d*)

I

Imre, Z. (*d*)
Inglesby, M. (*d*)
Ironside, C. & R. (*des*)
Ivanova, A. (*b*)

J

Jago, A. (*sm*)
James, F. (*d*)
James, T. (*d*)
Joffrey, R. (*ch*)
Jones, D. (*d*)
Jones, G. (*d-ch*)
Jones, L. (*d*)
Jouanneau, G. (*d*)
Judd, J. (*m*)
Julian, L. (*m*)

K

Kahn, S. (*sm*)
Kalichevsky, V. (*d*)
Karsavina, T. (*d*)
Katz, W. (*des*)

Kelly, A. (*d*)
Kelly, B. (*d*)
Kelly, G. (*des*)
Kelly, G.M. (*w*)
Kelly, J. (*d*)
Kemp, L. (*ch-des*)
Kemp, T. (*d*)
Kendall, C. (*m*)
Kern, H. (*d*)
Kernot, V. (*des*)
Kerr, M. (*d*)
Kerr, R. (*d*)
Kersley, L. (*d*)
Keuter, C. (*ch*)
King, A. (*w*)
Kingsley, C. (*mus*)
Kirkpatrick, S. (*des*)
Knott, A. (*d-ch*)
Koltai, R. (*des*)
Kornilof, N. (*des*)
Krassovska, N. (*d*)

L

Lacotte, P. (*ch*)
Laing, H. (*d-des*)
Lambert, J. (*comp*)
Landstone, C. (*m*)
Lane, M. (*d*)
Langfield, T. (*d*)
Larsen, G. (*d*)
Lascelles, A. (*d*)
Lavelle, M. (*d*)
Law, P. (*d*)
Law, G. (*m*)
Le Fanu, N. (*comp*)
Lendrum, A. (*d*)
Leslie, B. (*w*)
Lester, K. (*d-ch*)
Lewis, J. (*mus*)
Lidderdale, A. (*sm*)
Lillie, E. (*d*)
Linden, S. (*d*)
Lindsay, J. (*mus*)
Lingwood, T. (*des*)
Lishman, T. (*mus*)
Litster, T. (*d*)
Lloyd, M. (*d*)
Lock, E. (*d*)
Lockwood, A. (*comp*)
Longmuir, D. (*sm*)
Loretz, D. (*d*)
Low, J. (*sm*)
Loraine, I. (*d*)
Lorraine, M. (*d*)
Lubovitch, L. (*ch*)
Lucas, L. (*mus*)
Luzita, S. (*d*)
Lyall, C. (*d*)
Lynch, C. (*mus*)
Lyne, A. (*d*)

M

Maas, J. (*d*)
Macey, D. (*d*)

Mackay, C. (*d*)
Macfarlane, J. (*des*)
MacMillan, K. (*ch*)
MacSween, G. (*d*)
Manchester, D. W. (*m*)
Manley, C. (*sm*)
Mann, J. (*m*)
Marcuse, J. (*d*)
Markova, A. (*d*)
Marre, P. (*des*)
Marsh, V. (*d*)
Marshall, L. (*d*)
Martin, D. (*d*)
Martlew, G. (*d*)
Mason, T. (*m*)
Massey, G. (*d*)
Massie, A. (*m*)
McClelland, J. (*d*)
McCleod, K. (*m*)
McDowell, N. (*d-des*)
McGrath-Grogan, G. (*sm*)
Meadowcroft, M. (*d*)
Melis, P. (*d*)
Mellor, M. (*w*)
Mendel, D. (*ch*)
Merry, H. (*d*)
Metcalfe, J. (*comp*)
Metsis, I. (*d*)
Metters, C. (*mus*)
Miller, S. (*mus*)
Miranda, C. (*mus*)
Miskovitch, M. (*d*)
Molys, G. (*d*)
Montlake, E. (*des*)
Moore, G. (*ch*)
Moore, J. (*d*)
Morfield, S. (*d*)
Morgan, A. (*mus*)
Morrice, N. (*d-ch-dir*)
Morrison, A. (*mus*)
Morrison-Dixon, E. (*w*)
Morrison-Dixon, F. (*w*)
Morton, J. (*sm*)
Mumford, P. (*des*)
Munro, M. (*d*)
Murray-Clarke, I. (*des*)
Murrill, H. (*comp*)

N

Napier, J. (*des*)
Neumann, I. (*d*)
Newby, S. (*d*)
Newman, S. (*m*)
Newton, S. (*d*)
Nicholls, A. (*d*)
Nijinsky, K. (*d*)
Nobbe, W. (*des*)
Nordheim, A. (*comp*)
North, R. (*ch-dir*)
Norwood, A. (*d*)
Nystrom, N. (*d*)

O

Oakshott, J. (*sm*)
O'Brien, J. (*d*)
Oldham, A. (*comp-mus*)
Owen, S. (*d*)
Owens, E. (*d*)

P

Paltenghi, D. (*d-ch*)
Paoluzi, G. (*d*)
Pasley, P. (*d*)
Patrick, S. (*ch*)
Perez, C. (*d*)
Pieris, M. (*m*)
Pollen, M. (*d*)
Pomerantz, L. (*d*)
Poole, D. (*d*)
Preedy, C. (*mus*)
Prestidge, M. (*d*)
Price, A. (*d-b*)
Price, C. (*d*)
Pride, M. (*des*)
Prosser, J. (*w*)

R

Rabin, L. (*b*)
Racine-Fricker, P. (*comp*)
Rambert, M. (*d-Founder
    Director*)
Raphael, J. (*m*)
Rassine, A. (*d*)
Rawson, F. (*d*)
Read, J.B. (*ld*)
Recagno, E. (*d*)
Reed, M. (*mus*)
Reeder, K. (*sm-ld*)
Rees, S. (*d*)
Reeves, M. (*mus*)
Reid, R. (*d*)
Reid, S. (*m*)
Reyneke, D. (*d*)
Reynolds, I. (*d*)
Reynolds, D. (*d*)
Rianne, P. (*d*)
Ringwood, B. (*des*)
Rittman, S. (*d*)
Roberts, J.E. (*d*)
Roberts, S. (*w*)
Robertson, S. (*m*)
Robinson, A. (*m*)
Robinson, C. (*d*)
Roope, C. (*d*)
Rosenburg, D. (*d*)
Rowe, A. (*d*)
Rowell, K. (*des*)
Ruxton, E. (*d*)

S

Sacks, Q. (*d*)
Salaman, C. (*d*)
Salaman, M. (*d*)
Salaman, S. (*des-ch*)

Salzedo, L. (*mus-comp*)
Sandbrook, J. (*d*)
Sanders, J. (*d*)
Sarel, O. (*d*)
Scarlett, B. (*des*)
Schooling, E. (*d*)
Scoglio, J. (*d-ch*)
Scott, M. (*d-b*)
Semenova, T. (*d*)
Shelley, N. (*d*)
Sheppard, G. (*des*)
Sheringham, G. (*des*)
Sherwood, G. (*d-b*)
Shilton, G. (*sm*)
Short, S. (*d*)
Shute, H. (*m*)
Siegertsz, S. (*d*)
Siegfried, I. (*d*)
Singleton, S. (*d*)
Skeaping, M. (*d*)
Skene, P. (*m*)
Slavinsky. T. (*d*)
Sloan, C. (*m*)
Smith. A. (*d*)
Smith, B. (*d*)
Sokolow, A. (*ch*)
Some, D. (*d*)
Sopwith, N. (*d*)
Spartshott, A. (*d*)
Spaull, J. (*d*)
Speed, A. (*m*)
Spight, H. (*d*)
St. Claire, M. (*d*)
St. John, H. (*m*)
Staff, F. (*d-ch*)
Staples, J. (*d*)
Stevenson, H. (*des*)
Stewart, A. (*sm*)
Stewart, M. (*des*)
Stiff, W. (*m*)
Stimpson, K. (*m*)
Stokes, J. (*d*)
Stone, A. (*des*)
Stone, B. (*d-ch*)
Stuart, R. (*d*)
Sugihara, S. (*ch*)
Sutherland, L. (*m*)
Swinstead-Smith, E. (*des*)
Swithinbank, C. (*mus*)

T

Taylor, A. (*d*)
Taylor, J. (*d-ch*)
Taras, P. (*d*)
Ter-Arutunian, R. (*des*)
Tetley, G. (*ch*)
Thesmar, G. (*d*)
Thompson, A. M. (*m*)
Thomson, N. (*d*)
Thornborrow, B. (*m*)
Tillson, K. (*d*)
Toguri, D. (*ch*)
Toms, C. (*des*)
Toye, W. (*d-ch*)

Trailine, B. (*d*)
Trailine, H. (*d*)
Traill, M. (*d*)
Trunoff, V. (*d*)
Truscott, A. (*d*)
Tsakiris, J. (*d*)
Tucker, J. (*m*)
Tudor, A. (*d-ch*)
Tully, R. (*d*)
Turner, C. (*d*)
Turner, H. (*d*)

V

Valent, R. (*d*)
Van Dantzig, R. (*ch*)
Van Praagh, P. (*d*)
Van Schayk, T. (*des*)
Vandernoot, J. (*mus*)
Vardi, Y. (*d*)
Veillard, M. (*d*)
Verdy, V. (*d*)
Vincent, E. (*d*)
Vincent, H. (*mus*)
Vincent, P. (*d*)
Vine, L. (*m*)
Vlasic, P. (*d*)
Von Rosen, E.M. (*d*)
Voytek, (*des*)

W

Walden, M. (*d*)
Walker, D. (*d*)
Walker, H. (*d*)
Ward, E. (*d-b*)
Ward, O. (*w*)
Ward, S. (*w*)
Warren, L. (*d*)
Warwick, P. (*d*)
Webb, S. (*d*)
Webley, J. (*m*)
Wellesley, M. (*d*)
Westerdijk, L. (*d*)
Westlake, D. (*d*)
Whelan, C. (*comp*)
Wherlock, R. (*d*)
White, A. (*m*)
Whitley, A. (*choreologist*)
Whitworth, N. (*d*)
Wiles, J. (*d*)
Williams, M. (*d*)
Willis, M. (*d*)
Wilson, R. (*des*)
Wise, M. (*d*)
Wich, H. (*des*)
Woizikovsky, L. (*d*)
Wood, J. (*d*)
Wood, M. (*d*)
Wood, P. (*d*)
Woodward, C. (*d*)
Wooster, A. (*d*)
Wraith, M. (*d*)
Wright, B. (*d*)

Wright, P. (*d*)
Wylie, S. (*d*)

Y

Yamada, S. (*d*)
Yang, T. (*d*)
Yateman, K. (*d*)
Yerrell, R. (*d-ch*)
Yoshida, N. (*d*)

Z

Zolan, M. (*d*)

List of contributors

FREDERICK ASHTON: England's great choreographer, staged his first ballet at Marie Rambert's instigation in 1926, *A Tragedy of Fashion*. He did much of his important early work for Rambert. "She cultivated me" he once said, "She taught me musical appreciation, took me to museums, gave me books to read and recited endless Shakespeare and Racine at me". Ashton became Founder Choreographer for Sadler's Wells Ballet (later Royal Ballet) and Principal Choreographer from 1933–1970, succeeding Ninette de Valois as Director of the Royal Ballet 1963–1970, but has continued to create new works.

WILLIAM CHAPPELL: dancer, designer and director; adept in designing ballets economically for the small stage of the Mercury Theatre. Later joined the Vic-Wells Ballet and did equal service for them, designing Ashton ballets including *Les Rendezvous* and *Les Patineurs* (still used today), and also their early productions of classics like *Coppélia* and *Giselle*. During the war years he started writing dance criticism and published two books, *Studies in Ballet* and *Margot Fonteyn* (in 1951). He now works mostly as a director of plays, musicals and revues.

JOHN CHESWORTH: dancer, choreographer and director, joined Ballet Rambert in 1952 after eighteen months at the Rambert School of Ballet. He soon established himself as one of the finest and most versatile of character dancers. He choreographed his first work in 1966 and created seven ballets for the company repertoire. He has a consuming interest in film and television. Director of Ballet Rambert 1974–80.

MARY CLARKE: writer on ballet and editor since 1963 of *The Dancing Times*. Dance critic of *The Guardian*. Assistant editor and contributor of *The Ballet Annual* (1952–63). London editor of *Dance News of New York* (1955–70). Author of *The Sadler's Wells Ballet: a History and an Appreciation* (1955) and a companion volume, *Dancers of Mercury – The Story of Ballet Rambert* (1962). Contributor *Encyclopedia Britannica*. Since 1973 has collaborated with Clement Crisp on no fewer than seven books including *Design for Ballet* (1978) and *The History of Dance* (1981).

CLEMENT CRISP: lecturer, writer, ballet critic. Dance critic with *Financial Times* since 1957, author of many ballet books, several in collaboration with Mary Clarke. Librarian and archivist of The Royal Academy of Dancing since 1968.

NINETTE DE VALOIS: founder of the Sadler's Wells Ballet (later Royal Ballet), dancer, choreographer, director and teacher, used many of Rambert's dancers in her early stagings at Sadler's Wells and in turn loaned hers to the Ballet Club and Ballet Rambert. She choreographed one ballet for Ballet Rambert, *Bar aux Folies Bergère*, based on Manet's painting, to music by Chabrier with designs by William Chappell.

WILLIAM FERGUSON: Ballet Rambert's longest serving member of staff. Joining the company in 1948, he spent many arduous years touring at home and abroad as Stage Manager. When the company transformed itself into a modern dance company in 1966 he was appointed Chief of Production, a post he still holds today.

SALLY GILMOUR: one of the finest dramatic ballerinas of her generation; born in Malaya, came to England in 1930 where she studied with Tamara Karsavina and then at the Rambert School. She made her name as the wife in Andrée Howard's *Lady into Fox* (1939); created roles in several ballets by Walter Gore and was much acclaimed for her portrayal of Giselle in Rambert's Romantic production of 1946. Her exceptional choreographic memory has helped recent re-stagings of the early Rambert ballets, such as *Dark Elegies*.

NOËL GOODWIN: assistant editor for *Dance & Dancers* until 1980. Music and dance critic for *The Daily Express* since 1956–78. Now a free-lance critic; reviews regularly for *The Times*, *International Herald Tribune* and *Ballet News* (New York). Frequently broadcasts for the B.B.C.; is a Council Member of the Arts Council as well as being Chairman of its Dance Panel and Deputy Chairman of the Music Panel. In 1979 he wrote the book, *A Ballet for Scotland*, about 10 years of the Scottish Theatre Ballet.

WALTER GORE: dancer, choreographer, was discovered and given his first opportunities in these fields with Rambert from 1930 until 1935. Went briefly to the Vic-Wells Ballet, creating the role of the Rake in de Valois's *The Rake's Progress*. After war service returned to Rambert to create a number of ballets such as *Simple Symphony*, *Mr Punch, Winter Night*, and *Antonia* which gave his wife, Paula Hinton, a strong dramatic role. He subsequently had companies of his own and worked world wide, always with Paula Hinton. He died in Portugal of a heart attack in 1979.

NIGEL GOSLING: writer, critic, married to Maude Lloyd. Together they write ballet criticism under the name of Alexander Bland for *The Observer*. He is the author of several books on ballet, including Nureyev's biography in 1962 and a study of the Fonteyn-Nureyev partnership in 1979.

DIANA GOULD: trained with Lubov Egorova in Paris and with Rambert in London in the late 1920s. She created roles in Ashton ballets *Leda and the Swan* and *Capriol Suite* and later danced with the Ballet Russe Company of Colonel de Basil and with the Markova-Dolin Company. She retired from the stage after her marriage to Yehudi Menuhin.

MAUDE LLOYD: dancer, ballet critic; born in Cape Town, came to London to appear in some of the very earliest Rambert performances, and created several important roles in the ballets of Antony Tudor, notably *Jardin aux Lilas* and *Dark Elegies*. She danced with the Markova-Dolin company in the 1930s appearing in Nijinska's *Les Biches*. She also created the role of the Bride in Andrée Howard's ballet, *La Fête Etrange,* with the London Ballet in 1940. After her marriage to Nigel Gosling she retired from the stage but with him, as Alexander Bland, is now a ballet critic.

P.W. MANCHESTER: writer and editor, known to all her friends as Bill, published a best selling account of the Vic-Wells Ballet in 1942 on the strength of which Marie Rambert invited her to become secretary to Ballet Rambert two years later. In 1946 she left to found the magazine *Ballet Today*, which she edited until 1951. She then went to New York to become joint editor with Anatole Chujoy of *Dance News* (until 1969) and was co-editor of the second edition of his *Dance Encyclopedia* (1947). Now adjunct-professor of Dance History at University of Cincinnati College of Music.

ALICIA MARKOVA: England's first great classical ballerina, joined Diaghilev's Ballet Russe in 1925 until it broke up in 1929. Ashton used her in many of his early creations for the Ballet Club 1931–33 and she was as instrumental in establishing Ballet Rambert as she was later to be with the Vic-Wells (Royal) Ballet, 1933–35. With Anton Dolin they formed their own company. Also danced with Ballet Russe de Monte Carlo and Ballet Theatre in America and later became co-founder and ballerina of London Festival Ballet.

NORMAN MORRICE: dancer, choreographer and Director of Ballet Rambert and the Royal Ballet. Born in Mexico in 1931. At the age of six he moved to Scotland and first took up ballet in Nottingham some years later. He enrolled at the Rambert School in 1952 and with the company the following year. He choreographed his first ballet *Two Brothers* in 1958 and went to New York in 1961 to study with Martha Graham for one year. In 1966 he was appointed Associate Director of Ballet Rambert, to be appointed Artistic Director in 1970 until 1974. He was appointed Director of the Royal Ballet in 1977.

SALLY OWEN: started dancing at the age of 2 in Bristol, eventually attending the Bristol Academy of Dancing as a full time student at the age of 15. She trained at the Rambert School for three years, and joined Ballet Rambert in 1971. Since then she has become one of the company's leading dancers, creating major roles in all the main works in the repertoire. She has choreographed four works for the company workshops, two of which were taken into the main repertoire. She is married to Yutaka Yamazaki, a freelance documentary film maker.

ANYA SAINSBURY (ANYA LINDEN): dancer. Born Manchester, started her ballet training in Berkeley, California and on returning to England studied four years at Sadler's Wells School before joining the Royal Ballet in 1951. Became a ballerina in 1958. Married John Sainsbury in 1963 and has three children. Is a member of the Board of Royal Ballet School, Ballet Rambert, Theatre Museum Advisory Council, and serves on the British Council's Drama and Dance Advisory Committee; and has organized several charity ballet galas in aid of One Parent Families.

SACHEVERELL SITWELL: poet and writer, younger brother of Osbert and Edith, was a great admirer of the Diaghilev Ballet Russe and close friend of the ballet historian and bookseller, Cyril Beaumont. During the 1921 Diaghilev production of *The Sleeping Princess* he came to love the classic Petipa repertory and used to go to Marie Rambert's studio in the 1920s to see dances like the Aurora or Blue Bird pas de deux because only there could he find them in London.

GLEN TETLEY: Dancer and choreographer, trained with Martha Graham and Antony Tudor. In 1962 he formed his own company and made his choreographic debut with *Pierrot Lunaire* to Schoenberg music, later to become one of Ballet Rambert's most highly acclaimed works. Subsequently he was dancer, choreographer and Co-Director of Netherlands Dance Theatre, and now as a freelance choreographer his ballets are in the repertoire of all the major companies throughout the world including American Ballet Theatre, Australian Ballet, Royal Ballet, London Festival Ballet, Royal Danish Ballet and the Stuttgart Ballet of which he was Artistic Director from 1974 to 1976. He has always had a special relationship with Ballet Rambert for whom his works include *Ziggurat, Embrace Tiger and Return to Mountain, Rag Dances, Praeludium* and his first full-length work, *The Tempest*.

ANTONY TUDOR: dancer, choreographer for Ballet Rambert and whilst in that company created his two best known ballets, *Jardin aux Lilas (Lilac Garden)* in 1936 and *Dark Elegies* to a Mahler song cycle which is still in repertoires throughout the world. He has been one of the most influential figures in ballet in this century.

PEGGY VAN PRAAGH: dancer, teacher and director. Danced for Ballet Rambert from 1933–38 creating roles in the Tudor repertory, notably in *Jardin aux Lilas* and *Dark Elegies*. When Tudor left to form his London Ballet she went with him and after he went to America in 1939 she and Maude Lloyd held the company together until, for economic reasons, it merged with Ballet Rambert. She later joined Sadler's Wells Ballet where she danced leading roles but found her true vocation as a teacher and ultimately as Assistant Director of the Sadler's Wells Theatre Ballet where she encouraged such young choreographers as Cranko and MacMillan. She became Artistic Director of the Australian Ballet from 1963 until 1974 and she still frequently returns to that company to help mount classic ballets.

PETER WILLIAMS: editor, designer, writer and critic. Ballet designs include Taras's *Designs with Strings* (Metropolitan Ballet, 1948), Howard's *Selina* (SW Theatre Ballet, 1948) amongst others; author, *Masterpieces of Ballet Design* (1981). Assistant Editor, *Ballet* (1948–50); Founder/Editor *Dance & Dancers* (1950 until its demise in 1980). Ballet critic, *Daily Mail* (1950–53); deputy critic *The Observer* (1970–); contributed articles and reviews for many publications in Great Britain and internationally.

Member of British Council's Drama and Dance Advisory Committee since 1961, Chairman 1975–81. Member of Arts Council committees from 1965–80, Chairman of its Dance Panel 1973–80; responsible for dance section of Opera and Ballet Report 1966–69 which resulted in the development of dance theatre in Great Britain.

Founder/Chairman, Dancers Pensions and Resettlement Fund (1975–). Vice Chairman, Royal Ballet Benevolent Fund. Member of most committees concerned with dance. OBE 1971.

Ballet Rambert photographed at the Riverside
Studios, April 1981

1. Richard   Alston
2. Prudence Skene
3. John Webley
4. William Ferguson
5. Christopher Bruce
6. Carolyn Fey
7. Diane Walker
8. Quinny Sacks
9. Frances Carty
10. Paul Melis
11. Catherine Becque
12. Sally Owen
13. Dame Marie Rambert
14. Lucy Burge
15. Lucy Bethune
16. Nicholas Carr
17. Sid Ellen
18. Bridget Thornborrow
19. Jane Attenborough
20. Yair Vardi
21. Jenny Mann
22. Michael Ho
23. Cathrine Price
24. Kathy Chard
25. Hugh Craig
26. Jkky Maas
27. Robert North
28. Bill Hammond
29. Malcolm Glanville
30. Guy Detot
31. Stephen Ward
32. Norio Yoshida
33. Rebecca Ham
34. Elizabeth Cunliffe
35. Christopher Swithinbank
36. Sally Garbutt
37. Nelson Fernandez
38. Pete Hart
39. George Shilton
40. Laura Carr